Eyewitness

A NEW WINDMILL BOOK OF REPORTAGE

Edited by John O'Connor

Heinemann
New Windmills

Heinemann Educational Publishers
Halley Court, Jordan Hill, Oxford OX2 8EJ
A division of Reed Educational and Professional Publishing Ltd

OXFORD MELBOURNE AUCKLAND
JOHANNESBURG BLANTYRE GABORONE
IBADAN PORTSMOUTH (NH) USA CHICAGO

04 03 02 01
10 9 8 7 6 5 4 3 2

ISBN 0435 12532 X

'The Ghost of Blue Bell Hill', found on the *Fortean Times* website, http://www.fortean
times.com; reprinted with permission. 'UFO', from online *Gloucestershire Echo*, 12 June 2000;
reprinted courtesy of the *Gloucestershire Echo*. 'Seagull Attack', from online *Gloucestershire
Echo*, 12 June 2000; reprinted with permission of *The Citizen*. Extracts from *Scrapbook
1900–1914*, ed. Leslie Bailey, published 1957 by Frederick Muller; reprinted with permission of
The Random House Group. Extract 'Concordes Write Page of History on Atlantic' by Arthur
Reed, in *The Times*, 25 May 1976 © Times Newspapers Ltd 25 May 1976; used with permission.
Extract 'The Sinking of the *Titanic*' in the *New York Times*, 19 April 1912; reprinted with
permission of the *New York Times*. Extract by Michael Buerk from *I'll Never Forget The Day*,
ed. Bob Willey, published by Alan Sutton 1988; used with permission. Extract 'What it feels like
in space', from the *Manchester Guardian*, 14 April 1961; reprinted with permission of the
Manchester Evening News. Extract from *Death of a President*, by William Manchester © 1967,
renewed 1995 by William Manchester; reprinted by permission of Don Congdon Associates Inc.
Extract 'Roger Bannister Breaks Four-Minute Mile', by Jack Crump, taken from the *Daily
Telegraph*, 7 May 1954 © Telegraph Group Ltd; used with permission. Extract from *The Letters
of Edith Wharton*, published by Simon & Schuster 1988; reprinted with permission of the Estate
of Edith Wharton and the Watkins/Loomis Agency, New York. Extract 'Gas Attack', from
The Virago Book of Women and the Great War, by Pat Beauchamp, published by Virago;
reprinted with permission of David Higham Associates Ltd. Extracts from *Siegfried Sassoon
Diaries 1915–1918*, by Siegfried Sassoon, and *Memoirs of an Infantry Officer*, by Siegfried
Sassoon, published by Faber and Faber Ltd; reprinted with permission of the publishers.
Extract from *Yesterday's Witness*, by James Cameron © James Cameron 1979; reproduced by
permission of BBC Worldwide Ltd. Extract 'The Horrors of Buchenwald' from the *Manchester
Guardian*, 18 April 1945; reprinted with permission of the *Manchester Evening News*.
Extract 'Allies Invent Atomic Bomb: First Dropped on Japan', from the *Daily Express*, 7 August
1945; used with permission.

Illustrations by Jackie Hill at 320 Design: atomic bomb map – Kim Williams;
'Seagull Attack' – John Holder

Photos: Michael Buerk – Camera Press; Earth from space – Photodisc; Berlin Wall – Camera
Press; 1966 England football team – Camera Press; Live Aid – Popperfoto; German U-boat –
Camera Press; zeppelin – Camera Press

Cover design: PCP Design Consultancy
Cover photo: Science Photo Library/Scott Camazine
Typeset by ✒ Tek-Art, Croydon, Surrey
Printed and bound in the United Kingdom by Clays Ltd, St Ives Plc

Contents

Introduction for students

The extracts in this book all come under the heading of 'non-fiction'. That means that, unlike novels and short stories, which are made up ('fiction'), these are true accounts written by real people. Huge gas-filled balloons really did sail over this country during the Great War of 1914–18 on terrifying bombing raids, for example, and the accounts you will read here were written by the men who dropped the bombs, the pilots who tried to shoot them down and the innocent victims down below.

But not all the extracts are about life-and-death dramas. You will read about the car-park attendant who was attacked by a seagull, and share the excitement of standing in a crowd of thousands at Glastonbury, to describe just two of the extracts.

The activities at the end of each section are to help you understand the extracts a little better and find new ways of looking at them. By the time you have worked through them you should have a good idea of what makes a really strong eyewitness account.

I hope you will enjoy reading these extracts. You can start off with a chilling encounter with a ghost, understand Yuri Gagarin's emotions as the first man in space and end with the horrors of the first atomic bomb. In between you will share some strange and powerful experiences – I hope they will inspire you to write your own accounts of events you experience.

John O'Connor

Introduction for teachers

The revised National Curriculum for English includes the requirement for students to engage with a range of 'non-fiction and non-literary texts'. The National Curriculum divides this category into four areas, one of which is reportage. *Eyewitness* has been designed to meet the needs of the reportage requirement.

The extracts included in this collection have been carefully selected to interest and motivate Key Stage 3 students. The extracts have been arranged according to theme. This allows students to compare the different ways in which eyewitnesses have reported on strange phenomena, for example, or to view war from many different perspectives.

Following each themed section is a wide range of activities. These are tailored to explore each extract in line with the demands of the proposed Framework for Teaching English at Key Stage 3. There are also activities that allow for comparative work across the selection of extracts within a section.

Care has been taken to build in differentiation within each section. This is provided through the subject matter (from UFOs to the fall of the Berlin Wall); the varying difficulty of language (from popular sports writing to seventeenth-century prose); and in the activities themselves.

I hope you will find that *Eyewitness* is a valuable resource in helping to meet the non-fiction requirements for all your Key Stage 3 students.

John O'Connor

I couldn't believe my eyes

Every now and then someone appears in the news with an extraordinary story. We might believe them, or we might not; but whether they have been abducted by aliens, or witnessed a statue moving, they all have dramatic stories to tell. The reports are packed with details that the witnesses noticed at the time and which are designed to convince us of the truth of the encounter. The aliens were extremely tall with domed heads, they say; the statue wept real tears and nodded from time to time.

In this section are four such accounts, involving strange encounters with ghosts, UFOs, intelligent seagulls and – to prove that people have been reporting unbelievable experiences for a very long time – a seventeenth-century mermaid. Read the introductions and extracts which follow, before working through the activities on pages 9–14.

Extract 1: The ghost of Blue Bell Hill (page 3)

On 19 November 1965 there was a fatal car crash on Blue Bell Hill in Kent, in which three women died. In the years which followed, motorists reported many strange experiences in which ghostly figures appeared in their headlights. Three separate drivers reported knocking down a woman who had run into their path; while two others claimed that a woman had stared calmly into their eyes as they ran over her. Then people started seeing a different apparition: the figure of a witch-like old woman. This is a report about a Mr and Mrs Maiden who happened to be driving over the hill one night in January 1993 . . .

Extract 2: Seagull attack! (page 4)

As animal attacks go, this report is not in the *Jaws* class – no lives are lost and nobody runs shrieking in terror. But there is still something rather sinister about a bird which seems to be carrying a particularly nasty grudge against a single, innocent human victim. And even if the weapon isn't deadly, the bird's aim is!

Extract 3: UFO (page 6)

Have you ever seen a strange light in the sky that no one else noticed? If there was no obvious explanation for it, then your sighting was one of the many Unidentified Flying Objects, or UFOs, reported every year. If you do see something strange and unexplained, make sure that you can give as detailed an account as Jim Brace did when he spoke to his local newspaper. (Even better – get a photograph!)

Extract 4: Mermaid (page 7)

When sailors returned from the early voyages of discovery, they would bring back countless stories of the strange creatures that they had seen: dragons, leviathans (whales), unicorns and people whose heads grew beneath their shoulders. One of their favourites was the mermaid. Here is Richard Whitbourne, describing his sighting of a curious sea-creature off the coast of St John's, Newfoundland, in 1610.

Extract 1

THE GHOST OF BLUE BELL HILL

The family had come up from Aylesford, turning northward onto the Old Chatham Road at the Lower Bell crossroads (a location, again, that features as a reputed 'picking up' point for the ghostly girl hitch-hiker in the early history of the case). Some 300 yards (275m) further up, at Kit's Coty Cottage, the road makes a sweeping bend to the right. As the car started to turn into the bend, they saw a figure start across the road from right to left in front of them. Mr Maiden immediately slowed down.

'At first I thought it was [somebody in] a fancy dress costume,' said Mrs Maiden. 'It was wearing a long dress, very old-fashioned, that stopped mid-calf. It had a tartan shawl round the top and a bonnet with a brim.'

Mrs Maiden remembers remarking to her husband: 'Somebody's playing a prank.' But then the car's headlights fully illuminated the figure.

'It was like when you trap a rabbit in your headlights. It stayed dazed, hunched over without looking at us. As we got alongside it we were almost at a standstill. All of a sudden it was 4ft [1.2m] away from the car. It rounded on us really quickly and I saw the face. It was totally horrific . . . very small, black beady eyes. It was like a wizened face. The worst thing of all was the mouth. It opened and [it] was like an empty black hole.

'My mother was sitting directly behind me. At the same time I remember we said, "Oh, my God." ' . . .

Fortean Times

reputed: well-known

Extract 2

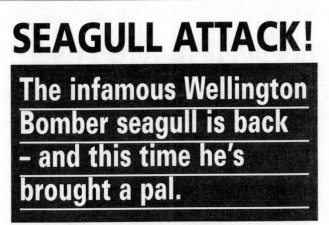

SEAGULL ATTACK!

The infamous Wellington Bomber seagull is back – and this time he's brought a pal.

The **psychotic** seagull has been singling out car park attendant Don Weston for aerial attacks over the last five summers. But now, as the bird dive-bombs the long-suffering Don at the Thomas Rich's car park off Wellington Street, Gloucester, another young gull flies in his wake. Six jumpers splattered with seagull droppings have already been relegated to Don's dustbin since the Wellington Bomber returned to Gloucester with reinforcements.

Gloucestershire's maddest seagull grabbed the media spotlight in 1998. Since then Don has written a children's book called *Swoop* about his experiences. 'He's not nasty any more – he's horrible,' said 56-year-old Don. 'He's exactly the same as he was before, and he knows me by my cough. When the seagull dive-bombs me, I duck out of the way. But as I get up again, his mate hits me on the head.'

NAUGHTY APPRENTICE

The new gull is a youngster with fluffy grey down among its feathers. It's not

---

psychotic: mentally disturbed

yet clear if the newcomer is a girlfriend or a naughty apprentice. Don said both gulls keep a look-out for him from the roof of a nearby building. 'The mate doesn't bomb me every time,' said Don. 'I should imagine he'll get better at it and it will be much worse for me this time next week.'

The Wellington Bomber has become so casual about the media attention, he will perform his spectacular dive-bomb for the cameras when Don calls him down.

DRIVEN TO ILLNESS

Don is currently off sick from his car park duties after suffering a bad bout of pneumonia during the winter. But he returns to Wellington Street every day to say hello to regular customers and talk to children. The car park attracts crowds especially to see the flying **phenomenon**.

But the Wellington Bomber is one summer regular Don could do without. 'He has sussed I'm moving slower than I used to and knows I'm an easy target,' said Don. 'He waits for me to get out of the car and attacks. Yet according to children, he's the hero these days and I'm the baddie.'

Gloucestershire Echo 12 June 2000

---

phenomenon: remarkable happening

Extract 3

GUARD JIM GETS AN EYEFUL OF UFO

Sky-gazing security guard Jim Brace is convinced he saw an enormous UFO and will not change his mind even if people make fun of him.

The 29-year-old was on patrol at the Unipart depot in South Littleton, near Evesham, just before midnight on Monday when he saw a huge object in the sky.

He then watched it for the best part of an hour.

Mr Brace, who said he did not believe in UFOs until the incident, said: 'It was partly cloudy and partly clear. This thing just gradually appeared. It looked like a plate, with small domes dotted all over it.

'Apart from ringing the police and my firm about it, I watched it the whole time.

'It was going round in circles every five minutes, although you could only see it clearly for 20 seconds each time.'

PC Tom Iddon said Evesham police would look into the matter. He said: 'We will keep an open mind but it may have been an advertising air balloon which I believe was in the area at the time.'

Mr Brace said he was sure it was nothing like a balloon, lights from a laser show or a plane.

He said: 'I've never seen anything like it and probably never will again.

'They could put me in a strait-jacket but I know what I saw and I won't change my mind for anything.

'It was massive and impossible to put a size on it. There was also no noise coming from it.'

Extract 4

Mermaid

1   Now also I will not omit to relate
something of a strange Creature that I
first saw there in the yeere 1610, in a
morning early as I was standing by the
5 water side, in the Harbour of Saint Johns,
which I **espied verie swiftly to come
swimming** towards me, looking cheerefully,
as it had beene a woman, by the Face, Eyes,
Nose, Mouth, Chin, eares, Necke and
10 Forehead: It seemed to be so beautifull, and
in those parts so well proportioned, having
round about upon the head, all blew **strakes**,
resembling haire, downe to the Necke (but
certainly it was haire) for I beheld it
15 long, and another of my companie also, yet
living, that was not then farre from me; and
seeing the same comming so swiftly towards
mee, I stepped backe, for it was come within
the length of a long **Pike**.
20 Which when this strange Creature saw that I
went from it, it presently thereupon dived a
little under water, and did swim to the place

---

espied verie swiftly to come swimming: saw swimming rapidly
as it had beene: as though it were
strakes: lines (like a boat's planks)
Pike: a weapon like a long spear

where before I landed; whereby I beheld the
shoulders and backe downe to the middle, to
25 be as square, white and smooth as the backe
of a man, and from the middle to the **hinder
part**, pointing in proportion like a broad
hooked Arrow; how it was proportioned in
the forepart from the necke and shoulders, I
30 know not; but the same came shortly after
unto a Boat, wherein one William
Hawkridge, then my servant, was, that hath
bin since a Captaine in a Ship to the East
Indies, and is lately there **imploied** againe by
35 Sir Thomas Smith, in the like Voyage; and
the same Creature did put both his hands
upon the side of the Boate, and did strive to
come in to him and others then in the said
Boate: whereat they were afraid; and one of
40 them **strooke** it a full blow on the head;
whereat it fell off from them: and afterwards
it came to two other Boates in the Harbour;
the men in them, for feare fled to land: This
(I suppose) was a Mermaide.

Richard Whitbourne, *Discourse and Discovery of
Newfoundland*, 1622

---

hinder part: rear of the body
imploied: employed
strooke: struck

Activities

1 **a** The way in which Mrs Maiden describes the ghostly figure in 'The Ghost of Blue Bell Hill' (page 3) helps to get across the family's growing terror. Her description can be divided into six sections, as in the table below. Re-read what she says and then write down the phrase which starts off each section. To help you, one of them has been filled in:

Section	Opening phrase of section
1 Mrs Maiden's first impression	
2 Description of the figure's clothes	
3 Mrs Maiden's reactions	Mrs Maiden remembers remarking . . .
4 Description of how the figure was standing	
5 Sudden movement from the figure	
6 Details of the face.	

b Write an extract from a ghost story which includes the moment when the ghostly figure is first seen. Divide the account up into six sections, similar to the ones describing the ghost of Blue Bell Hill. You could use a story that you have heard from the area where you live, or make one up of your own. Use language designed to build up suspense and tension in the same way as the Blue Bell Hill story.

c Do you believe in ghosts? Discuss this question in groups of four, keeping notes of the points that other people make. Then write an article for a magazine in which you express your own view and the views of the other three people. Make sure that you include as much evidence as you can to support all the opinions.

2 a Jim Brace's story about a UFO (page 6) is reported here in a local newspaper. Read it again and notice how the article is put together. The writer has:

- created an eye-catching headline
- given us the most important fact in the first paragraph (called 'the introduction')
- introduced the main point of the story early in the article (in the second and third paragraphs)
- included some eyewitness statements from Jim Brace
- given us a different point of view with comments from PC Tom Iddon.

Count how many lines (approximately) the writer has devoted to each of these five sections. Which one takes up most of the article? Draw a rough pie-chart to show what proportion of the article each of the five sections takes up.

b Write your own newspaper article about a person who sees a strange, unidentified animal prowling around their local streets. It should have:

- an eye-catching headline

- a short introduction giving the main facts ('Gardener Mrs Joyce Collins was amazed when …')
- an introduction to what actually happened ('The retired teacher was weeding her herb garden when …')
- quotes from an eyewitness ("It wasn't an ordinary cat," said Mrs Joyce. "For one thing, it had …")
- a quote from someone else, such as a police officer or an official from the local zoo ("We've had several reports like this …").

c   What do you think about UFOs? Are they extraterrestrial visitors or can they normally be explained away by weather balloons or aircraft? Write a letter to a newspaper or a notice for a website in which you express your opinion. Make sure that you include as much evidence as you can to support your views.

3   a   Don Weston's experiences as described in 'Seagull attack!' (pages 4–5) would make an excellent animated film in the style of *Chicken Run!* Draw a series of rough sketches to represent a storyboard for part of the film. For example, you could choose the events described on page 44 ('"He's exactly the same … hits me on the head."').

First, make a note of what should appear in each frame. You might start like this:

> *Frame 1: Don comes out of his attendant's hut and puts his cap on. He coughs . . .*

b   We are told that Don Weston has written a children's book about his experiences with the Wellington Bomber, called *Swoop*. Write the opening two or three pages (no more than 150 words) of your own story about a mischievous animal, aimed at young children. Remember to keep the story and the language clear and simple.

c The way this piece is written implies that the seagull's behaviour is deliberate yet crazy. Pick out three words and phrases that give this impression.

4 **a** Richard Whitbourne's account of a mermaid (pages 7–8) was written nearly four hundred years ago, and since that time there have been many changes to the English language. Look first at some of the changes which have taken place in English spelling:

- *Final 'e'* The word 'beene' (line 8) no longer has an 'e' at the end; how many other words can you find in the passage which we would not spell with a final 'e'?
- *Double letters* 'Beautifull' (line 10), like other words ending in *–ful*, no longer takes a double letter at the end; find other examples of words in the account which Richard Whitbourne spelled with double letters and you would spell with a single letter.

What other differences do you see between modern English and early seventeenth-century English?

b Turn Richard Whitbourne's account into an item for Newfoundland Radio, 1610. Write it out as a radio script, starting with an introduction, and leading into an interview with Whitbourne himself. You can write in modern English or, if you are feeling confident, imitate the language of the early seventeenth century, using Whitbourne's spellings and some of his vocabulary. When your script is ready, perform it in small groups.

Comparing texts

5 **a** How does each of these writers make their report convincing and readable? Look back through the extracts and find examples of each of the features in the left-hand column of the table below. When you have found some, copy and complete the chart below. Two examples have been given already, to start you off.

	The ghost of Blue Bell Hill	UFO	Seagull attack!	Mermaid
Vivid descriptive details of appearance				
Vivid descriptive details of behaviour				
Quotes from an eyewitness				
Detailed facts and figures	it was 4ft [1.2m] away from the car			
Comparisons with well-known things				like a broad hooked Arrow
Humour				

b Write your own account of a strange and
troubling encounter. It might be a sighting of (or
a meeting with …) a ghost, a mystery creature
or a UFO.

To make your account come alive, use some of
the features you have identified in question 5a.

Section 2
Success!

It is fortunate for us that some of mankind's greatest achievements have been recorded for all time, by witnesses or by the inventor or adventurer themselves. In this section you can read reports of the first radio signal to be sent across the Atlantic, the first powered flight across the English Channel and the first supersonic passenger flight from London to the American capital, Washington. Read through the introductions and extracts which follow, before working through the activities on pages 23–26.

Extracts 1 and 2: Signals across the Atlantic (pages 17 and 18)

When Guglielmo Marconi sent a radio signal from one side of the Bristol Channel to the other in 1897, not many people were interested. But they soon took notice when he set up his apparatus in two ships and reported what was happening in the America's Cup yacht race, in 1899. Suddenly Marconi was famous. But scientists still refused to believe that radio signals could travel great distances, until a dramatic day in December 1901. This extract tells how Marconi himself reported the great moment. Having set up a transmitter in Poldhu, in Cornwall, he and his assistant Kemp tensely awaited a signal in a small hut built on the cliffs of Newfoundland, in Canada.

Marconi's achievement was reported in newspapers throughout the world. The second account is written by a journalist from *The Times*: his account took two days to reach London!

Extract 3: Flying the Channel (page 19)

Inspired by the Wright brothers' first powered flight in 1902, the Frenchman Louis Blériot determined to be the first to fly across the English Channel. This is his account of that flight, undertaken in the summer of 1909.

Extract 4: Concorde (page 21)

In 1909 Blériot's 28-horsepower monoplane had averaged 46 miles per hour, and took 40 minutes to carry one man across the English Channel. By 1976 an airliner could carry passengers across the Atlantic at speeds faster than sound. This was Concorde, an aircraft developed jointly by the French and the British to cross the Atlantic in under three hours. Among its first group of passengers was a journalist writing for *The Times*.

Extract 1

Signals across the Atlantic

Shortly before mid-day I placed the single earphone to my ear and started listening. The receiver on the table before me was very crude — a few coils and **condensers and a coherer** — no valves, no amplifiers, not even a crystal. But I was at last on the point of putting the correctness of all my beliefs to the test. The answer came at 12.30 when I heard, faintly but distinctly, **pip-pip-pip**. I handed the phone to Kemp: 'Can you hear anything?' I asked. 'Yes,' he said, 'the letter S' — he could hear it. I knew then that all my anticipations had been justified. The electric waves sent out into space from Poldhu had **traversed** the Atlantic — the distance, enormous as it seemed then, of 1,700 miles — **unimpeded by the curvature** of the earth. The result meant much more to me than the mere successful realization of an experiment. As Sir Oliver Lodge has stated, it was an **epoch** in history. I now felt for the first time absolutely certain that the day would come when mankind would be able to send messages without wires not only across the Atlantic but between the farthermost ends of the earth.

**Marconi Guglielmo, from *Scrapbook 1900–1914*
ed. Leslie Bailey**

---

condensers and a coherer: instruments for storing electric charges and detecting electric waves
pip-pip-pip: the letter S in Morse Code (written as *dot dot dot*). It is no longer used, but for a long time the international emergency signal (SOS) was represented in Morse code by *dot dot dot*, *dash dash dash*, *dot dot dot*
traversed: crossed
unimpeded by the curvature: the curve of the earth's surface had not prevented the signal from getting through
epoch: beginning of an important period

Extract 2

WIRELESS TELEGRAPHY ACROSS THE ATLANTIC

St. Johns, N.F., DEC. 14.

Signor Marconi authorizes me to announce that he received on Wednesday and Thursday electrical signals at his experimental station here from the station at Poldhu, Cornwall, thus solving the problem of telegraphing across the Atlantic without wires. He has informed the Governor, Sir Cavendish Boyle, requesting him to **apprise** the British Cabinet of the discovery, the importance of which it is impossible to overvalue.

Signor Marconi is informing the Italian Government himself. He states that the signals were necessarily faint, but they were conclusive. He returns next week to England, where he will assume charge of the Poldhu station himself, increasing the power of the electric generators and sending stronger signals to his assistants here, who remain for the purpose of receiving them.

The Times, 16 December 1901

---

apprise: inform

Extract 3

Flying the Channel

In the early morning of Sunday, 25 July 1909, I left my hotel at Calais and drove out to the field where my aeroplane was garaged. On the way I noted that the weather was favourable to my **endeavour**. I therefore ordered the destroyer *Escopette*, placed at my disposal by the French Government, to go to sea. I examined my aeroplane. I started the engine, and found it worked well. At half-past four we could see all round. Daylight had come. My thoughts were only upon the flight, and my determination to accomplish it this morning.

Four thirty-five. *Tout est prêt!* In an instant I am in the air, my engine making 1,200 revolutions – almost its highest speed – in order that I may get quickly over the telegraph wires along the edge of the cliff. As soon as I am over the cliff I reduce my speed. There is now no need to force my engine. I begin my flight, steady and sure, towards the coast of England. I have no **apprehensions**, no sensations, *pas du tout*. The *Escopette* has seen me. She is driving ahead across the Channel at full speed. She makes perhaps 26 miles per hour. What matters? I am making over 40 mph. Rapidly I overtake her, travelling at a height of 250 feet. The moment is supreme, yet I surprised myself by feeling no exultation. Below me is the sea; the motion of the waves is not pleasant. I drive on. Ten

---

endeavour: difficult attempt
Tout est prêt!: Everything is ready!
apprehensions: worries
pas du tout: not at all

minutes go. I turn my head to see whether I am proceeding in the right direction. I am amazed. There is nothing to be seen – neither the destroyer, nor France, nor England. I am alone. I am lost.

Then I saw the cliffs of Dover! Away to the west was the spot where I had intended to land. The wind had taken me out of my course. I turned and now I was in difficulties, for the wind here by the cliffs was much stronger, and my speed was reduced as I fought against it. My beautiful aeroplane responded. I saw an opening and I found myself over dry land. I attempted a landing, but the wind caught me and whirled me round two or three times. At once I stopped my motor, and instantly my machine fell straight on the ground. I was safe on your shore. Soldiers in khaki ran up, and also a policeman. Two of my **compatriots** were on the spot. They kissed my cheeks. I was overwhelmed.

Louis Blériot, from *Scrapbook 1900–1914*
ed. Leslie Bailey

Afterword:
Blériot's 28-horsepower aircraft averaged 46 miles per hour, making the crossing in 40 minutes. It was later exhibited at the London department store Selfridges, and 120,000 people filed past it in four days.

---

compatriots: people from my own country (Frenchmen)

Extract 4

Concorde writes page of history over the Atlantic

Washington, 24 May

British Airways and Air France Concordes opened the **supersonic era** across the North Atlantic today when they flew to Washington from London and Paris respectively in just under four hours – half the normal **subsonic** airliner time.

The Air France aircraft touched down at Dulles International Airport 1½ minutes after the British Airways Concorde, as the British aircraft was turning off the runway.

Environmentalists, who had at one time threatened to block the start of the service, made only a minimal protest at each end today, handing out leaflets and displaying anti-Concorde notices at Heathrow and Dulles.

Concorde now has a 16-month trial period, approved by the United States Government, in which to prove that it is not the noisy beast many Americans think it is.

I was among the 75 passengers, 35 of them fare-paying, at £352 single compared with the £291 first-class single fare by subsonic jet, when the British Airways Concorde, registration G-BOAC, pushed away exactly on time from the Heathrow terminal at lunchtime today.

supersonic era: a period when objects can travel faster than the speed of sound
subsonic: slower than the speed of sound

The Concorde rolled slowly to the end of the runway where the airliner's commander, Captain Brian Calvert, aged 42, announced that we would hold for six minutes so that takeoff would be **synchronized** with that of the Air France Concorde from Paris.

At precisely one minute past 1 pm there was the now familiar roar as Captain Calvert opened the throttles of the four Rolls-Royce Olympus engines and we leapt forward down the runway.

Captain Calvert kept us informed of our progress as we levelled out at 26,000 ft at just below the speed of sound, so that there was no sonic boom on the ground below.

'This is the first time the brave little bird has been allowed to go to America', he said. After 19 minutes from takeoff he was back on the cabin address system to announce that we were going supersonic – 630 miles an hour.

As we climbed to our cruising height of 55,000 ft, with the sky above a deep blue, Captain Calvert informed us that the air temperature outside was minus 54°F and that the fuselage had heated up to 97°F.

The halfway point across the North Atlantic, 30°W, was reached after we had been flying for 1 hour and 18 minutes.

Two hours and 50 minutes out of London, flying 10 miles high at over 1,000 mph, we began our descent into Washington. Three hours and 52 minutes out of London we touched down smoothly at Dulles Airport.

The Times, 24 May 1976

---

synchronized: made to happen at the same time

Activities

1   a   Look back at the two texts about the first radio signals sent across the Atlantic (pages 17–18). The first was written by Marconi himself and is in the first person ('I placed . . .', 'I was at last . . .'). The second article was written by a journalist about Marconi's achievement and is in the third person ('He has informed the Governor . . .', 'He states that . . .').

Here is a section of Marconi's text with another version beside it, rewritten in the third person. Study the two versions carefully and then answer the questions which follow.

Original version (in the first person)	New version (rewritten in the third person)
The answer came at 12.30 when I heard, faintly but distinctly, *pip-pip-pip*. I handed the phone to Kemp: 'Can you hear anything?' I asked. 'Yes,' he said, 'the letter S' – he could hear it.	*The answer came at 12.30 when he heard, faintly but distinctly, pip-pip-pip. He handed the phone to Kemp and asked him whether he could hear anything. Kemp replied that he could: the letter S.*

When you change a piece of writing from the first person into the third person:

- What happens to the first person pronoun ('I')?

- What happens to the verb in direct speech ('Can')?
- Which words have to be added?

What are the strengths and weaknesses of each version?

b Imagine that Marconi's great breakthrough happened only yesterday. Use the information from the two extracts to write a front-page article for a tabloid newspaper. Think up a dramatic headline and use an atlas to sketch a map which will help readers to picture where the places are. Include quotes from Marconi and his assistant Kemp.

   You might find it helpful to look back at the advice on writing newspaper articles (pages 10–11). As this is for a tabloid, make sure you have a sensational logo, a dramatic, eye-catching heading and lots of sub-headings.

2 a Study Louis Blériot's account of flying across the English Channel (pages 19–20). When people draft an account of something that they have done, they usually write in the past tense (I *got* up early . . . *travelled* to the station . . . *bought* a ticket . . .). Blériot, however, switches tenses in this account: sometimes he writes in the past and sometimes in the present.

- Which tense does he begin with?
- Where does he change tense?
- Where does he change back again?

Why do you think he decided to change tenses like this? What is special about the section that he has written in the present tense?

b Write a short account of a dramatic journey. Write it in the first person (see question 1a) and, to make it more exciting and interesting to read, change tenses. You could use this frame (which outlines an expedition up Mount Everest) as a structure.

Section	What happens	Person	Tense
Introduction	*You leave base camp.*		*Past tense*
Paragraph 2	*You begin the climb.*		*Past tense*
Paragraph 3	*Suddenly a snowstorm blows up.*	First person	*Present tense*
Paragraph 4	*You struggle to survive.*		*Present tense*
Paragraph 5	*The storm dies down.*		*Past tense*
Conclusion	*You get to the summit.*		*Past tense*

3 **a** The journalist writing the article about Concorde's first flight for *The Times* (pages 21–22) clearly wanted to include as many facts and statistics for his readers as he could. To get an idea of how important the facts are, answer the following questions:

- There were two Concordes flying to Washington simultaneously: which cities did they come from?
- Which aeroplane touched down first?

- How long was the trial period given for Concorde to prove that it was not a noise hazard?

Work out three more factual questions and then, in pairs, see if you can answer each other's questions.

In the same pairs, decide what you think are the ten most important facts in this article.

b On your own, use the ten facts to write a short entry on Concorde for a children's encyclopaedia. Make it as interesting as you can, but make sure that all your facts are accurate.

Comparing texts

4 Do some research on a dramatic and important human achievement and then write an 'eyewitness' account of it. You could write about:

- an expedition, such as the first circumnavigation of the globe, or the first people to reach the South Pole
- a scientific breakthrough, such as the discovery of radium or the development of penicillin
- a technological advance, such as the building of the first steam engine, or the invention of television.

You might want to write about someone you have been learning about in other lessons (such as History, Science, Geography or RE).

Decide whether you are going to write in the first person (as if you had personally experienced the events), or in the third person.

Your account could be in the form of a newspaper article (like those on Marconi and Concorde) or a personal account (like Marconi's or Blériot's).

Section 3
Disaster

Human history has seen many disasters. The most powerful reports have often been from people who were caught up in the catastrophic events. These extracts start with a description of the ruins of San Francisco after the earthquake in 1906 and end with an account of the 1984 famine in Ethiopia. The middle extract gives two accounts of the sinking of the *Titanic* in 1912. Read the introductions and extracts which follow, before working through the activities on pages 34–37.

Extract 1: The San Francisco earthquake (page 28)

On 17 April 1906, San Francisco was devastated by a terrible earthquake. Many died and 225,000 people were made homeless. In this extract the writer Jack London describes the awful scenes of devastation.

Extract 2: The sinking of the *Titanic* (page 30)

This one of the best known of all disasters. The 'unsinkable' liner had only 1,178 lifeboat places for the 2,224 people aboard, and 1,513 lives were lost after the ship struck an iceberg. Here are two accounts: the first is by Harry Senior, a fireman working on the ship, and the second by one of the passengers, Mrs D.H. Bishop.

Extract 3: Famine in Ethiopia (page 32)

Michael Buerk is a BBC journalist. In 1984 he reported on the famine which had hit Ethiopia. This and other accounts by Michael Buerk and his team led to the famous Live Aid charity appeal.

Extract 1

The San Francisco Earthquake

At half-past one in the morning three sides of Union Square were in flames. The fourth side, where stood the great St Francis Hotel, was still holding out. An hour later, ignited from top and sides, the St Francis was flaming heavenward. Union Square, heaped high with mountains of trunks, was deserted. Troops, refugees, and all had retreated.

It was at Union Square that I saw a man offering a thousand dollars for a team of horses. He was in charge of a truck piled high with trunks from some hotel. It had been hauled here into what was considered safety, and the horses had been taken out. The flames were on three sides of the square, and there were no horses.

Also, at this time, standing beside the truck, I urged a man to seek safety in flight. He was all but hemmed in by several **conflagrations**. He was an old man and he was on crutches. Said he: 'Today is my birthday. Last night I was worth thirty thousand dollars. I bought five bottles of wine, some delicate fish, and other things for my birthday dinner. I have had no dinner, and all I own are these crutches.'

I convinced him of his danger and started him limping on his way. An hour later, from a distance, I saw the truckload of trunks burning merrily in the middle of the street.

On Thursday morning, at a quarter past five, just twenty-four hours after the earthquake, I sat on the steps of a small residence of Nob Hill. With me sat Japanese, Italians, Chinese, and Negroes – a bit of a

---

conflagrations: destructive fires

cosmopolitan **flotsam** of the wreck of the city. All about were the palaces of the **nabob pioneers of Forty-nine**. To the east and south, at right-angles, were advancing two mighty walls of flame.

I went inside with the owner of the house on the steps of which I sat. He was cool and cheerful and hospitable. 'Yesterday morning,' he said, 'I was worth six hundred thousand dollars. This morning this house is all I have left. It will go in fifteen minutes.' He pointed to a large cabinet. 'That is my wife's collection of china. This rug upon which we stand is a present. It cost fifteen hundred dollars. Try that piano. Listen to its tone. There are few like it. There are no horses. The flames will be here in fifteen minutes.'

Outside, the old Mark Hopkins residence, a palace, was just catching fire. The troops were falling back and driving refugees before them. From every side came the roaring of flames, the crashing of walls, and the detonations of dynamite.

I passed out of the house. Day was trying to dawn through the smoke pall. A sickly light was creeping over the face of things. Once only the sun broke through the smoke pall, blood-red, and showing quarter its usual size. The smoke pall itself, viewed from beneath, was a rose colour that pulsed and fluttered with lavender shades. Then it turned to mauve and yellow and dun. There was no sun. And so dawned the second day on stricken San Francisco.

Jack London, *Collier's Weekly*, 5 May 1906

---

flotsam: the people are compared with floating wreckage
nabob pioneers of Forty-nine: people who had made a fortune out of the 1849 gold rush

Extract 2

The Sinking of the *Titanic*

Harry Senior

*I was in my bunk when I felt a bump. One man said, 'Hello. She has been struck.' I went on deck and saw a great pile of ice on the well deck before the **forecastle**, but we all thought the ship would last some time, and we went back to our bunks. Then one of the firemen came running down and yelled, 'All muster for the lifeboats.' I ran on deck, and the Captain said, 'All firemen keep down on the well deck. If a man comes up I'll shoot him.'*

Then I saw the first lifeboat lowered. Thirteen people were on board, eleven men and two women. Three were millionaires, and one was Ismay [J. Bruce Ismay, Managing Director of the White Star Line; a survivor].

Then I ran up on to the hurricane deck and helped to throw one of the collapsible boats on to the lower deck. I saw an Italian woman holding two babies. I took one of them, and made the woman jump overboard with the baby, while I did the same with the other. When I came to the surface the baby in my arms was dead. I saw the woman strike out in good style, but a boiler burst on the Titanic and started a big wave. When the woman saw that wave, she gave up. Then, as the child was dead, I let it sink too.

Mrs D.H. Bishop

We did not begin to understand the situation till we were perhaps a mile or more away from the Titanic. *Then we could see the rows of lights along the decks begin to slant gradually upward from the **bow**. Very slowly the lines of light began to point downward at a greater and greater angle. The*

---

forecastle: the front part of a ship (pronounced fo'c'sle)
bow: the front end of a ship

sinking was so slow that you could not perceive the lights of the deck changing their position. The slant seemed to be greater about every quarter of an hour. That was the only difference.

In a couple of hours, though, she began to go down more rapidly. Then the fearful sight began. The people on the ship were just beginning to realize how great their danger was. When the forward part of the ship dropped suddenly at a faster rate, so that the upward slope became marked, there was a sudden rush of passengers on all the decks towards the **stern**. It was like a wave. We could see the great black mass of people in the **steerage** sweeping to the rear part of the boat and breaking through into the upper decks. At the distance of about a mile we could distinguish everything through the night, which was perfectly clear. We could make out the increasing excitement on board the boat as the people, rushing to and fro, caused the deck lights to disappear and reappear as they passed in front of them.

This panic went on, it seemed, for an hour. Then suddenly the ship seemed to shoot up out of the water and stand there perpendicularly. It seemed to us that it stood upright in the water for four full minutes.

Then it began to slide gently downwards. Its speed increased as it went down head first, so that the stern shot down with a rush.

The lights continued to burn till it sank. We could see the people packed densely in the stern till it was gone ...

As the ship sank we could hear the screaming a mile away. Gradually it became fainter and fainter and died away. Some of the lifeboats that had room for more might have gone to their rescue, but it would have meant that those who were in the water would have swarmed aboard and sunk her.

Harry Senior and Mrs D.H. Bishop in the *New York Times*, 19 April 1912

stern: the rear part of a ship
steerage: the cheapest accommodation on the ship

Extract 3

Famine in Ethiopia

I'll never forget the day that I found out what desperate hunger is really like for so many millions of people, who live on the very borders of existence.

My camera team and I had been filming the results of the Ethiopian famine. We had spent several days watching people die in front of us, children as well as adults, and seen tens of thousands of poor Ethiopians who did not seem far away from that fate. We were, I realize now, in a mild state of shock. So much horror around; such an enormous scale of suffering.

It was a **paradox** of this famine that when we went into a village in the middle of the worst affected area we found a café of sorts that was not only open but sold Coca-Cola and bread rolls. We sat in the corner of this mud room and were about to have these things for breakfast when there was a commotion at the door.

There must have been several hundred starving people fighting for a chance to see somebody eating.

At the very front was an old man, lined and wiry. His eyes were wide and his hands were trembling. He fell to his knees and, very slowly, started to move towards us across the floor with both hands stretched out, begging, in front of him.

Who could have eaten under those circumstances? But what could we do? We gave the old man some

---

paradox: the opposite of what you would expect

bread and went out into the street and, in a pathetic sort of way, tried to break up the rolls to feed all those people.

I have never felt so useless and I'm sure my colleagues felt the same. There was really nothing any of us could say to each other for some time after.

Michael Buerk, *I'll Never Forget the Day*, 1988

Activities

1 **a** In his description of the sights he witnessed in
the aftermath of the San Francisco earthquake
(pages 28–29), Jack London brilliantly gets
across, not only how devastating the earthquake
had been to the city's buildings, but also how
great the losses were to human beings.

In your own words, write brief descriptions
(not more than 40 words) of:

- the man in charge of the truck piled high with
  trunks
- the old man on crutches
- the owner of the house on whose steps Jack
  London had been sitting.

In pairs, talk about which of these three you feel
most sorry for, and why.

b Imagine that television had been invented in
1906 and that the cameras were recording the
destruction of San Francisco. Select quotations
from the extract which can be put together to
make a script for Jack London to read on the
news. Alternatively, imagine that you are making
a documentary about the event, and use
quotations as the basis for a commentary.
Sketch out two or three frames to show what
the viewers might see. Part of the news story or
the commentary can include the words spoken
by the three men Jack London quotes.

For example, an opening frame might show the
buildings of Union Square on fire, with Jack London
saying: 'At half-past one in the morning ...'

  c Jack London uses powerful words like `ignited`
    and `flaming heavenward` to express the force
    of the fires and the devastation that they
    caused. Pick out three more examples of these
    expressions to describe the fire and try to
    explain the impression they create.

2 a Re-read the first account of the sinking of the
    Titanic (page 30), by Harry Senior. His account
    is powerful because it is written in a very simple
    style: he shows that you do not need to fill your
    sentences with adjectives and adverbs in order
    to tell a dramatic story. There are hardly any
    adjectives in his account. He writes about a
    great pile of ice and a *big* wave; and refers to
    collapsible boats and an *Italian* woman; but
    most sentences have no adjectives at all.

    • one adjective is repeated near the end of
      Harry Senior's account: what is it?
    • do you think the account would be equally
      effective if there were no other adjectives?
      Why, or why not?

  b The impact of Harry Senior's account comes
    mainly through the verbs. In pairs, use the
    following list of verbs to retell the opening few
    moments of the story:

      I *was* … I *felt* … *has been struck* … I *went* …
      we all *thought* … *would last* … we *went* back

    Write out a list of the verbs which he uses to tell
    the next part of the story.

  c Imagine that you are a survivor of the disaster.
    Select information from the two accounts (pages
    30–31) and write a letter to one of your relatives
    at home, giving them some idea of how

terrifying the ordeal has been. Your letter should be about 100 words long.

3 **a** In order to tell this part of his story (pages 32–33) clearly and simply, Michael Buerk divides it into seven short paragraphs. Re-arrange these seven headings so that they match up with the order of the paragraphs:

- the café
- the old man
- introducing the story
- the reaction of Michael Buerk and the camera team
- feelings the camera team were left with afterwards
- the reaction of the starving people
- setting the scene.

b Use the details from Michael Buerk's account to create the front page of a campaign leaflet which is trying to raise money to help starving people in Ethiopia. Think about the main image (you might find something suitable in a magazine) and the language you want to use, in order to persuade people to donate money.

c Michael Buerk manages to communicate the horror and extent of the famine very clearly in this report. Pick out the words and phrases that you think are most successful in achieving this effect and explain why you have chosen them.

Comparing texts

4 **a** In pairs, look back through the extracts in this section and decide which one impressed you most. You might find it helpful to ask yourself the following questions:

- Which of the three disasters did I personally feel most involved in after reading the extracts?
- Which extracts taught me something I didn't know before?
- Which of the reports seemed to get across the scale of the disaster most effectively?
- Which one made me understand how the disaster affected individuals?
- Which writer's use of language was most effective?
- Which single moment in all the reports did I find most memorable?

b Choose a disaster from history and write a report as though you were an eyewitness. Remember:

- you will need to do some research on what happened, using books, magazines and the Internet
- when you have done the research, decide which moments in the disaster you are going to focus on
- you should plan your report carefully, so that it follows a logical order
- some of the best eyewitness reports are written very simply and tell their story through the verbs, rather than the adverbs and adjectives.

Section 4
Momentous times

People have always known how important it is to record the dramatic happenings that take place in the world around them. This section includes reports on three very different events which were to have a lasting and world-wide impact: the first manned space flight; the assassination of the President of the United States, John F. Kennedy; and the breaching of the Berlin Wall. Read the introductions and extracts which follow, before working through the activities on pages 50–52.

Extract 1: Man in space (page 40)

In the 1950s the Soviet Union was leading the race to be the first nation to send a man into space. After successes with Sputnik, the first artificial satellite to orbit the Earth in October 1957, and a second successful flight a month later, this time with a dog on board, the Soviet scientists decided that the time was right to plan a manned mission. In April 1961 the cosmonaut Yuri Gagarin – whose surname means 'wild duck' – became the first human being in space. In this report from the *Manchester Guardian*, he describes the view from space and the strangeness of his experiences.

Extract 2: The assassination of President Kennedy (page 44)

The assassination of John F. Kennedy was such an earth-shattering event that almost anybody who was over the age of five at the time can tell you exactly where they were and what they were doing when they heard of his death.

By 1963 Kennedy, the youngest ever President of the United States, had become an enormously popular figure and people were hopeful that he would become a great world leader. But in November of that year he was killed by a gunman, Lee Harvey Oswald, while on a visit to Dallas. Oswald was himself murdered soon afterwards and nobody has yet been able to discover who was really behind the assassination of President Kennedy.

When William Manchester decided to write his account of the shooting, he tried to tie together all the eyewitness accounts that he could collect. This extract from his book begins with the slow progress of the motorcade taking Kennedy through the streets of Dallas. Suddenly there was a sharp, shattering sound . . .

Extract 3: The fall of the Berlin Wall (page 47)

After the end of the Second World War in 1945, a period known as 'the cold war' began. This was a time when communist countries (led by the Soviet Union) and the countries of the West (such as Britain and America) were deeply suspicious of each other. It did not help that Germany had been divided in two: a communist part (East Germany) and a capitalist part (West Germany). The former capital, Berlin, lay in East Germany but was itself divided into East and West Berlin. West Berlin was linked to the rest of West Germany by a single road and railway running across East Germany, but giving no access to it. In 1961 communist East Germany started to construct a massive wall in Berlin to separate East Berlin from West Berlin, which thus became completely cut off from all links with East Germany. The Berlin Wall, as it came to be known, lasted until the fall of communism in 1989, and over a hundred people were killed trying to escape over it to West Berlin. This report, from the German newspaper *Die Welt* ('The World'), describes one of the first moments leading up to the removal of the Wall.

Extract 1

What it feels like in space

Gagarin burst out singing for joy

The moon next stop?

Moscow

Major Yuri Gagarin described today how it felt to be the first man in space – how he was able to write and work and how he burst out singing for joy as his ship plunged back towards the earth.

'Everything was easier to perform. . . legs and arms weighed nothing,' he told a Soviet interviewer. Objects swam about in the cabin and he actually sat suspended above his chair in mid-air, gazing out in admiration at the beauty of the earth floating in a black sky.

'I ate and drank and everything was like on earth,' he went on. 'My handwriting did not change, though the hand was weightless. But it was necessary to hold the writing-block as otherwise it would float away from the hands . . .' The passage from weightlessness to gravitation was gradual and smooth as he descended.

He had wanted to be a space traveller. 'The wish to fly in space was my own personal wish. When I was given this task, I began to prepare for the flight, and as you see, my wish has come true.'

Describing his feelings during the flight, Major Gagarin said: 'I was entirely concentrated on carrying out the flight programme. I wanted to carry out every point of the assignment and to do it as well as possible. There was a lot of work. The entire flight meant work.'

He stressed that he had no feeling of isolation in space. 'I knew well,' he said, 'that my friends, the entire Soviet people, were following my space flight. I was sure that the party and the Government would always be ready to help me if I found myself in a difficult situation.'

Saw collective farms

Describing how the earth looks from space, he said: 'The sunlit side of the earth is visible quite well, and one can easily distinguish the shore of continents, islands, great rivers, large areas of water, and folds of the land.' Flying over Soviet territory he saw distinctly the great squares of the fields of collective farms, and could tell what was ploughland and what was meadowland.

'Before this I had never been above 15,000 metres (49,213 feet). From the spaceship satellite one does not, of course, see as well as from an aeroplane, but very, very well all the same. During the flight I saw for the first time with my own eyes the earth's spherical shape. You can see its curvature when looking to the horizon.

'I must say the view of the horizon is quite unique and very beautiful. It is possible to see the remarkably colourful change from the light surface of the earth to the completely black sky in which one can see the stars. This dividing line is very thin, just like a belt of film surrounding the earth's sphere. It is of a delicate blue colour. And this transition from the blue to the dark is very gradual and lovely. It is difficult to put it in words.

In mid air

'When I emerged from the shadow of the earth the horizon looked different. There was a bright orange strip along it, which again passed into a blue hue and once again into a dense black colour.

'I did not see the moon. The sun in outer space is ten times brighter than here on earth. The stars are visible very well: they are bright and distinct. The whole picture of the heavens is much more contrasty than when seen from the earth.'

When weightlessness set in, he felt excellent. 'Everything was easier to perform,' Major Gagarin said. 'This is understandable. Legs and arms weigh nothing. Objects are swimming in the cabin, and I did not sit in the chair, as before, but was suspended in mid air. During the state of weightlessness I ate and drank and everything was like on earth.

'I was working in that state, noting my observations. Handwriting did not change, though the hand was weightless. But it was necessary to hold the writing block, as otherwise it would float away from the hands. I was in communication contact on various channels, using a telegraph key.

Smooth transition

'I was convinced that weightlessness has an effect on the ability to work. The passage from weightlessness to gravitation, to the appearance of the force of gravity, happens smoothly. Arms and legs feel as previously, the same as during weightlessness, but now they have weight. I ceased to be suspended over the chair, but eased myself into it.

'When I returned to the earth I was overjoyed. I was warmly met by our Soviet people. I was moved to tears by Nikita Sergeyevich Khrushchev's telegram. I was moved by his **solicitude**, interest, warmth. My greatest joy came when I spoke by telephone to Khrushchev and (President) Brezhnev. My heartfelt gratitude, my **filial thanks** to Nikita Sergeyevich for his solicitude for my person.'

Regarding the United States' intention to send a man into space, he said: 'We shall welcome the successes of the American cosmonauts when they have flown. There is room in space for everybody. Our party and Government are posing the question of peaceful exploitation of space, of peaceful competition. Space should not be used for military but peaceful purposes. The American cosmonauts will have to catch up with us. We shall welcome their successes, but we shall try to be always ahead.'

Manchester Guardian, 14 April 1961

Afterword:

Yuri Gagarin became a hero to the Soviet people, but only seven years later he was killed while testing a new aircraft. He was buried with full honours alongside the Soviet Union's most famous leaders in Red Square, in Moscow.

---

solicitude: concern
filial thanks: like the thanks that a son might give to his father

Extract 2

The Assassination of President Kennedy

On Main Street Ted Clifton said, 'That's crazy, firing a salute here.' Godfrey McHugh said, 'It *is* silly.'

In the VIP bus Dr Burkley was staring out absently at store windows. The President's physician had heard nothing. He was too far back.

The President was wounded, but not fatally. A 6.5 millimetre bullet had entered the back of his neck, bruised his right lung, ripped his windpipe, and exited at his throat, nicking the knot of his tie. Continuing its flight, it had passed through Governor Connally's back, chest, right wrist, and left thigh, although the Governor, suffering a delayed reaction, was not yet aware of it. At the moment, in fact, Connally was glancing over his right shoulder in the direction of what he had recognized as a rifle shot.

As the **Lincoln** emerged from behind the freeway sign, it re-appeared in Abe Zapruder's line of vision. Abe saw the stifled look on the President's face and was stunned. Continuing to train his camera on the car, he wondered whether Kennedy could be pretending. It was as though he were saying, 'Oh, they got me.' Abe thought, *The President is to joke?*

Nellie Connally twisted in her seat and looked sharply at Kennedy. His hands were at his throat, but he wasn't grimacing. He had slumped a little.

Lincoln: a model of car

Roy Kellerman thought he had heard the President call in his **inimitable** accent, 'My God, I'm hit!' Roy looked over his left shoulder – Greer, beside him, was looking over his right shoulder; the car, wobbling from side to side, slowly veered out of line – and they saw that Kennedy *was* hit.

At this instant the impact of John Connally's wound hit him. It was as though someone had jabbed him in the back with a gigantic fist. He pitched forward, saw that his lap was covered with blood, and toppled to the left, towards his wife. Both John and Nellie were aware that the Lincoln was slowing down. Huddled together, they glanced up and saw the astounded faces of Kellerman and Greer, inches from their own.

Suddenly the Governor felt doomed. He panicked.

'No, no, no, no!' he shrieked. 'They're going to kill us both!'

Jacqueline Kennedy heard him. In a daze she wondered, *Why is he screaming?*

Already she had started to turn anxiously to her husband.

Greer turned back to the wheel. Kellerman, hesitant, glanced over his shoulder again. Neither had yet reacted to the crisis.

And now it was too late. Howard Brennan, open-mouthed, saw Oswald take deliberate aim for his final shot. There was an unexpected, last-moment distraction overhead. The first shot had alarmed the birds. As the sound **ricocheted** in the amphitheatre below, the band-tailed pigeons had begun to depart, first in twos and threes, then in swarms, until now there were a thousand wings flapping overhead, rising higher and higher until they had formed a great ragged

---

inimitable: impossible to imitate; unique
ricocheted: echoed from one building to the next (pronounced 'rick-o-shayed')

fluttering fan overhead, a deep blue V blending into the gentler blue of the overarching sky.

Oswald squeezed the trigger.

The **First Lady**, in her last act as First Lady, leaned **solicitously** towards the President. His face was **quizzical**. She had seen that expression so often, when he was puzzling over a difficult press conference question. Now, in a gesture of infinite grace, he raised his right hand, as though to brush back his tousled chestnut hair. But the motion faltered. The hand fell back limply. He had been reaching for the top of his head. But it wasn't there any more.

William Manchester, *The Death of a President,* 1967

First Lady: the wife of the President (Jacqueline Kennedy)
quizzical: he had a comical, puzzled expression

Extract 3

At Brandenburg Gate, Police from East and West protect the Wall

It began a few hours after the announcement of the freedom to travel. Helping hands from above continually pulled people up to the top of the concrete wall. In front of the **Brandenburg Gate**, which represents both the separation of Germany as well as the desire for unity, the Wall is only 2.5 metres tall, but to the surprise of all it is about 3.5 metres thick. A short while ago, none of the demonstrators would have expected to get so close to the Brandenburg Gate.

From here one can see right into the majestic street, Unter den Linden, in the heart of East Berlin. About 200 East Berliners and other curious East Germans were standing there the whole day, looking towards the West. Many were saying it was time that this entrance was opened. In comparison to the West, however, the mood here was more subdued.

On Friday there were initially only 70 members of the **DDR** Border police standing between the Gate and the Wall itself, looking towards the West. They were young men from 20–25 years old, and their stony glances were beginning to lighten up. For the first time in the history of the Wall they had to prevent a mass attempt to cross from the West.

In true Berliner style, schoolchildren of 10 to 14 years, having received the day off school on this historical day, demanded to be let through. At least some demonstrators had

DDR: German Democratic Republic, the former East Germany
Brandenburg Gate: the main opening in the Berlin Wall

succeeded in penetrating from the West through to Alexanderplatz in the East the previous night.

A Border guard with dark skin became the darling of the occupants of the Wall. First he accepted two red carnations which a young girl gave him. She had just jumped off the Wall into the East. The young man kept the two flowers in his hand for a while. Hundreds of others jumped from the Wall into the East as well, and tried to sprint through the Gate. But all of them were stopped by the East Berlin Border guards, and lifted back onto the Wall.

With the coming of darkness, the mood changed. Older demonstrators also appeared on the Wall, and **Sekt and Schnapps** bottles began to circulate freely.

The East Berlin Border troops began to bring in reinforcements. About 300 Border guards stood in a long chain. Behind the Gate, which was lit up by car headlights from both East and West, military lorries formed an additional chain. There was a good reason for this: by now there were approximately 200 to 300 young people on the foreground of the Brandenburg Gate, which is still called Hindenburg-Platz as a **remnant of the West**. The people called up to those standing on the Wall 'Jump down! Jump down!'. The West Berlin police warned the demonstrators through loudspeakers to be careful. But few people took the threats seriously. Finally, on Saturday at 3 a.m. the Eastern troops began to force the mass of demonstrators back in the direction of the Wall. As that did not seem to work, they tried to pick out individuals every so often and lift them back up.

At the south end of the Hindenburg Platz, where the Wall is 3.5 metres tall, the sounds of hammers were heard for hours. The young people succeeded at breaking

---

Sekt and Schnapps: alcoholic drinks
remnant of the West: the name had survived the division of Berlin

off some of the round concrete blocks, and dropping them over into **the death strip** in the East. As dawn arrived one of the upper parts of a concrete plate reinforced with steel broke off, amid much cheering. It was only when the West Berlin police announced over loudspeakers that 'Symbolic removals of the Wall are useless. Please remain calm.', and threatened the use of force, that the thousands hesitatingly retreated.

Anette Wirth and Frank Pawassar, *Die Welt,*
3 November 1989

Afterword:
The Berlin Wall finally came down on 9 November 1989;
East and West Germany were unified in October 1990

---

the death strip: a strip of land along the Wall on the communist side. If anyone entered it, they were shot

Activities

1 a Re-read the extract about the first manned space
      flight on pages 40–43. Use the information in the
      article to write an 'interview' column for a
      magazine. The column might begin with a few
      background facts, followed by questions, like this:

      Yuri Gagarin
      • First human being in space, April 1961

         Q: Have you always wanted to be a
             space traveller?
         A: Yes, the wish to fly in space was my
             own personal wish.

   b This is a news report from the *Manchester
      Guardian* about Yuri Gagarin's experience of
      space. It contains a great many details from
      Gagarin. What techniques of layout and
      structure does it use to lead the reader through
      all the detailed information and keep his or
      her attention?

2 a To write his account of Kennedy's assassination
      (pages 44–46), William Manchester collected all
      the eyewitness accounts he could find, and used
      information from many of them.
      What did he learn from:

      • Nellie Connally (about Kennedy's position
        immediately after he had been shot)?
      • Roy Kellerman (about Kennedy's last words)?
      • the First Lady (about the expression on her
        husband's face and his final movement)?

   What information did Howard Brennan provide?

b Use the main points from William Manchester's account as the basis for a front-page newspaper article to be published the day after the assassination. Remember to include:

- an eye-catching headline
- a short introduction giving the main facts ('President Kennedy has been assassinated …')
- an introduction to what actually happened ('On the final day of his visit to Dallas …')
- quotes from eyewitnesses ('"I heard a gun-shot," said eyewitness Ted Clifton …')
- a quote from someone else, such as the police ('"The shots came from …"').

3 a Look back at the German newspaper article on pages 47–49. It is different from the first two extracts because it has no quotes from people who were present. Instead, it gives a series of pictures.

To get an idea of how 'pictorial' the writing is, imagine you are a member of a television crew recording these historic events. Use the descriptions in the article as the commentary for the six or seven main images you want to include on today's news. Then draw a sketch of each image and write the commentary underneath. For example, you might start with an image of young people being pulled up onto the Wall, with the commentary: 'It began a few hours after the announcement of the freedom to travel. Helping hands from above continually pulled people up to the top of the concrete wall.'

b Imagine that you are the Border Guard who was given two red carnations by the young girl. Write your diary entry for that day. Try to get across both the historical importance of the event and your own feelings.

c This article is written in the third person and the past tense, which makes the event seem more distant. Rewrite it as if you are a member of a TV crew observing things as they happen. To give your piece a more immediate effect, write in the first person, use the present tense and include interviews with people taking part.

Comparing texts

4 a These three extracts are all reports of important historical events, but the writers take different approaches to their subjects. In pairs, talk about the following questions:

- Which extract is made up mainly of quotes? Why do you think the writer decided to include so much quotation?
- Which extract contains the most facts and figures? Why are they important?
- Which extract draws upon the reports of several different eyewitnesses? Why is it useful to have so many viewpoints?

b Choose one of these three events and write an entry for a history book aimed at young children (you can decide the age-range of the readers yourself). You will need to:

- concentrate on the main points – leave out technical details
- write simply and clearly – avoid difficult vocabulary
- keep the article fairly short.

Section 5
The big event

Every now and then we might be lucky enough to be part of a crowd that is witnessing a stunning stage performance or some great sporting triumph. For us, and for millions of others, moments like this are the big event. Read the introductions and extracts which follow, before working through the activities on pages 69–74.

Extract 1: Joe Louis – world champion (page 55)

In 1937 a young black boxer called Joe Louis became heavyweight champion of the world. A year later he defended his title against the only man who had ever beaten him – the German Max Schmeling. Louis never took fights personally, but this one was different: not only had Schmeling been saying nasty things about him in the press, but he was a staunch supporter of Hitler and the Nazis. Louis had something to prove . . .

Extract 2: The final of '66 (page 58)

Wembley Stadium has seen some thrilling football matches. Jason Tomas recalls the last time England won a major football trophy: the final of the 1966 World Cup.

Extract 3: Bannister beats the record (page 61)

If you were to ask people to draw up a list of the most memorable sporting achievements, many would include the one-mile race at the Iffley Road track in Oxford, in 1954. This was the occasion on which a young medical student called Roger Bannister broke through one of the greatest barriers in athletics – the four-minute mile. His time of 3 minutes 59.4 seconds still stands as an amazing achievement. Here is the report from the *Daily Telegraph*, published the day after the race, and a brief account by the journalist David Harding.

Memories of Live Aid and Glastonbury

For many people, the biggest events they can remember are not sporting moments, but rock concerts. Neill Bayley and Lucy O'Connor recall two memorable musical events fifteen years apart.

Extract 4: Memories of Live Aid (page 65)

In July 1985 the rock musician Bob Geldof organised Live Aid, a major charity event in support of famine relief in Africa. At that time it was history's biggest pop concert, involving 63 acts playing on both sides of the Atlantic, in Wembley Stadium and Philadelphia. Neill Bayley worked as part of the stage crew at the Wembley Stadium.

Extract 5: Memories of Glastonbury 2000 (page 67)

The Glastonbury Festival in 2000 was said to have been one of the best ever, featuring performers such as David Bowie and Travis. But for 16-year-old Lucy the main attraction was the Wailers, backing band of the legendary Bob Marley.

Extract 1

Joe Louis – World Champion

Listen to this, buddy, for it comes from a guy whose palms are still wet, whose throat is still dry, and whose jaw is still agape from the utter shock of watching Joe Louis knock out Max Schmeling.

It was a shocking thing, that knockout – short, sharp, merciless, complete. Louis was like this:

He was a big lean copper spring, tightened and retightened through weeks of training until he was one **pregnant** package of coiled venom.

Schmeling hit that spring. He hit it with a whistling right-hand punch in the first minute of the fight – and the spring, tormented with tension, suddenly burst with one **brazen spang** of activity. Hard brown arms, propelling two **unerring** fists, blurred beneath the hot white candelabra of the ring lights. And Schmeling was in the path of them, a man caught and mangled in the whirring claws of a mad and feverish machine.

The mob, biggest and most prosperous ever to see a fight in a **ball yard**, knew that here was the end before the thing had really started. It knew, so it stood up and howled one long shriek. People who had paid as much as $100 for their chairs didn't use them – except perhaps to stand on, the better to let the sight burn forever in their memories.

There were four steps to Schmeling's knockout. A few seconds after he landed his only punch of the fight,

---

pregnant: full, ready to spring
brazen spang: powerful burst
unerring: never making any mistakes
ball yard: baseball stadium

Louis caught him with a lethal little left hook that drove him into the ropes so that his right arm was hooked over the top strand, like a drunk hanging to a fence. Louis swarmed over him and hit with everything he had – until Referee Donovan pushed him away and counted one.

Schmeling staggered away from the ropes, dazed and sick. He looked drunkenly toward his corner, and before he had turned his head back Louis was on him again, first with a left and then that **awe-provoking right** that made a crunching sound when it hit the German's jaw. Max fell down, hurt and giddy, for a count of three.

He clawed his way up as if the night air were as thick as black water, and Louis – his nostrils like the mouth of a double-barrelled shotgun – took a quiet lead and let him have both barrels.

Max fell almost lightly, **bereft of** his senses, his fingers touching the canvas like a comical **stew-bum** doing his morning exercises, knees bent and the tongue lolling in his head.

He got up long enough to be knocked down again, this time with his dark unshaven face pushed in the sharp gravel of the **resin**.

Louis jumped away lightly, a bright and pleased look in his eyes, and as he did the white towel of surrender which Louis' handlers had refused to use two years ago tonight came sailing into the ring in a soggy mess. It was thrown by Max Machon, **oblivious to** the fact that fights cannot end this way in New York.

---

awe-provoking right: a punch with the right hand that gave you feelings of fear and wonder

bereft of: deprived of

stew-bum: comic tramp

resin: the surface of the canvas floor

oblivious to: forgetting or unmindful of

The referee snatched it off the floor and flung it backwards. It hit the ropes and hung there, limp as Schmeling. Donovan counted up to five over Max, sensed the **futility** of it all, and stopped the fight.

The big crowd began to rustle restlessly toward the exits, many only now accepting Louis as champion of the world. There were no eyes for Schmeling, sprawled on his stool in his corner.

He got up eventually, his dirty grey-and-black robe over his shoulders, and wormed through the happy little crowd that hovered around Louis. And he put his arm around the Negro and smiled. They both smiled and could afford to – for Louis had made around $200,000 a minute and Schmeling $100,000 a minute.

But once he crawled down in the belly of the big stadium, Schmeling realized the implications of his defeat. He, who won the title on a partly **phony foul**, and beat Louis two years ago with the aid of a crushing punch after the bell had sounded, now said Louis had fouled him. That would read better in Germany, whence earlier in the day had come a cable from Hitler, calling on him to win.

It was a low, sneaking trick, but a rather typical last word from Schmeling.

Bob Considine, *International News Service*, 22 June 1938

Afterword:
Louis defended his title a total of 25 times, more than any other boxer.

---

futility: uselessness
phony foul: Schmeling had previously won the title by claiming that his opponent had fouled him

Extract 2

The Final of '66

Alf Ramsey, a man noted for not showing his emotions, showed a self-restraint remarkable even by his standards on the afternoon of 30 July 1966. At the final whistle in his England team's World Cup final against West Germany, Ramsey was approached by the trainer, Harold Shepherdson, who tried to lift him off his touchline seat. Ramsey was unmoved. 'Sit down, Harold,' he commanded.

It's a pity that others were not able to follow his example. England's 4–2 victory, sealed in a gripping 30 minutes of extra time, created so much excitement that the St John's Ambulance Brigade members on duty at the match reported several cases of fainting – even heart attacks – amongst the 100,000 crowd. As an estimated 400 million watched this epic contest on TV,

the mind boggles at what the overall total of suitable cases for treatment – psychological as well as physical – could have been. But who would have wanted to miss the sight of Ramsey's troops, controversially pushed into action with no orthodox winger and no **Jimmy Greaves**, producing the greatest two hours in English soccer history?

The memory has remained particularly vivid in East London, given the impact of Ramsey's West Ham trio of Bobby Moore, his **imperious** central defender and captain; Martin Peters, a player whose **versatility** caused Ramsey to describe him as being '10 years ahead of his time'; and striker Geoff Hurst, who justified his inclusion at the expense of Greaves by becoming the first player to score a World Cup final hat-trick.

With Hurst having cancelled out Helmut Haller's opening goal for Germany, Peters put England ahead initially 13 minutes from the end of normal time. But in the last minute, England suffered another blow when Wolfgang Weber brought the teams level again. The England players inevitably looked shattered, yet before the start of extra time, Ramsey, later to be knighted, implored them: 'You have beaten them once, now do it again. Look at them. They're more tired than you are.'

Ten minutes into extra time, Hurst hit the underside of the bar with a shot from a cross by the **indefatigable** Alan Ball. The ball bounced almost

---

Jimmy Greaves: then England's most successful goal-scorer, left out of Ramsey's team

imperious: Moore gave orders in a very forthright way

versatility: ability to play in different positions and employ different styles

indefatigable: the West Germans could not exhaust Ball

straight back down. Hurst and Hunt, who was following up, wheeled away, arms raised, claiming the goal. But did the ball cross the line? The goal stood, sparking a **controversy** that still rages to this day. Deep into the last minute, with Germany giving the whole home nation **palpitations** with their efforts to save the game, Moore hit a long ball into the path of Hurst on the halfway line. Hurst somehow summoned the strength to go forward with it . . . and then hit an explosive left-foot shot into the roof of the net. No mistake there. England had won, 4–2. 'They think it's all over,' observed the BBC's match commentator, Kenneth Wolstenholme, referring to spectators on the pitch as Hurst was about to swing his boot at the ball. 'It is now,' he added.

Jason Tomas, *Great Sporting Moments*

---

controversy: argument, dispute
palpitations: irregular heartbeats

Extract 3

ROGER BANNISTER BREAKS FOUR-MINUTE MILE

◆

Time of 3min 59.4sec is Triply Checked

From Jack Crump

OXFORD, Thursday

The first four-minute mile in the history of athletics was accomplished here to-day by Roger Gilbert Bannister, 25-year-old medical student, who was timed officially to run the distance in 3min 59.4sec. This was two seconds faster than the world record of Gundar Haegg, of Sweden, made in 1945.

This great triumph by an English athlete on an English track – Bannister ran on the Iffley Road ground, where he learned his running as an undergraduate – took the sporting world by surprise. It came at the start of an athletic season in America and in Europe, where several runners, notably John Landy (Australia), Joseph Barthel (Luxembourg), who beat Bannister in the 1952 Olympic Games, and Wes Santee (U.S.) planned final assaults on the 'even time' mile. Landy, who has done 4min 2sec, is soon to make an attempt in Finland.

When Bannister ran a mile in 4min 2sec at Motspur Park last year it was disallowed as an official record in this country because of technical non-compliance with the required conditions.

There is no danger, however, of his time this evening failing to be ratified by the International Amateur Athletic Federation.

Three official timekeepers

certified the time and the race, which was run in a properly constituted match between the **A.A.A.** and Oxford University, was on a track which measured half an inch more than the required 440 yards.

The world record application form has been completed by officials of the British Amateur Athletic Board, who will formally submit the performance for ratification without delay.

POOR CONDITIONS

Bannister's historic run was all the more remarkable because it was his first public race this season, and the chilly and blustering wind, varying between 15 and 25 m.p.h., made conditions far from ideal for record breaking.

HOW RACE WAS WON
Brasher Sets Pace

Luckily the weather improved, and it was learned when the six runners in the race went to the starting line that

Bannister and his great friend, C.J. Chataway, were to attempt to run a really fast mile.

The competitors, in addition to Bannister and Chataway, were the Olympic steeplechaser, C.W. Brasher, W.T. Hulatt of Alfreton, the Northern Counties champion, and two Oxford runners, G.P. Dole and A.D. Gordon.

From the start it was Brasher who went out in front, followed by Bannister and Chataway, and it was obvious that the pace was correct if a new world record were to be achieved. Brasher was leading slightly at the end of the first quarter-mile in 57.4sec, with Bannister a yard behind in 57.5sec and Chataway in third position in 57.6sec.

Brasher nobly assumed the role of pacemaker, and at the half-mile stage led in 1min 58sec, with Bannister clocked at 1min 58.2sec, with Chataway in third place ⅕th of a second slower.

A.A.A.: Amateur Athletic Association

After two and a half laps Brasher, having done his self-allotted task splendidly, faltered, but immediately Chataway sprang forward to take over the lead. At the bell, with three-quarters of a mile covered, Chataway was one yard ahead of Bannister in 3min 0.4sec Bannister's official time being 3min 0.5sec.

At once the cheering crowd realised that the historic four-minute mile was an exciting probability. All round the last lap the crowd roared encouragement to the runners, and when Chataway slowed with 250 yards to go, Bannister strode into the lead, quickly opened a gap and, appearing not even to be strained, sprinted to the tape in fine style and broke it to win in 3min 59.4sec.

He was exhausted as he stumbled from the track, but quickly recovered on learning that he had achieved the world's first

HAEGG AND BANNISTER
LAP BY LAP

This is how the world record miles of Bannister (3min 59.4sec) and Gundar Haegg of Sweden (4min 1.4sec in 1945) compare:

	Bannister	Haegg
1st lap	57.5sec	56.6sec
2nd lap	60.7sec	61.9sec
	(1min 58.2)	(1min 58.5)
3rd lap	62.3sec	61.2sec
4th lap	58.9sec	61.7sec

This was Bannister's progress: 220 yds 28.7sec, 440 yds 57.5sec, 660yds 1min 27.5sec, 880 yds 1min 58.2sec, 1,100 yds 2min 29.6sec, 1,320 yds 3 min 0.5sec, 1,540yds 3min 30.4sec

four-minute mile. He had also established a new world, British Empire, British national, British all-comers, European, English native and a whole string of other records.

Chataway finished in second place in 4min 7.2sec and Hulatt third in 4min 16sec. Once again Chataway had unselfishly run a magnificent race in support.

RAN AS PLANNED

1,500 Metre Prospects

I spoke to Roger Bannister soon after the race and he told me that the intermediate lap times of 57.5sec, the half-mile in 1min 58.2sec and the three-quarter mile in 3min 0.5sec were almost exactly what he had hoped.

He expressed the greatest delight, not merely on being the first man to achieve the coveted distinction, but also of having performed this feat on the track of the University where he was athletic president.

Bannister's time was taken at the 1,500 metres mark by one watch and was returned at 3min 43sec, which is equal to the world record time standing to the credit of the Swedish runners, Gundar Haegg and Lennart Strand, and the German, Werner Lueg. But since there were not the recognised number of timekeepers specifically timing at this intermediate distance, it cannot go forward as equalling the world record.

Unquestionably in my view a new 1,500 metres record is something which Bannister confidently may look forward to achieving this season – an important season in view of the Empire and European Games later in the summer.

Daily Telegraph, 7 May 1954

Afterword:

Just a few weeks later, Bannister's record was broken by the Australian runner John Landy. But, though his record did not last, his achievement is in the history books.

Extract 4

Memories of Live Aid

I have only snapshot memories of the music on the day. Elvis Costello's cover of *All You Need is Love* seemed brilliant for its simplicity; the power of U2; the **charisma** of Freddy Mercury; the emotional wrench of the video reminding us of why we were there while Bowie's *Heroes* played; all of these things live on alongside the failure of Bob Geldof's microphone during *I Don't Like Mondays* and Paul McCartney's during *Let It Be*. Hell, at least we were on schedule!

There was one moment I will also treasure personally which occurred after the UK transmission. The sound crew were seated at the front of the stage for a brief rest before **breaking the set,** when I saw a totally exhausted Bob Geldof crossing behind us. I

---

charisma: attractive personality which comes across powerfully
breaking the set: taking down the stage and everything on it

moved over with my hand outstretched to shake his and to thank him for what he had done. Ignoring my hand, he simply hugged me like a brother and thanked us all (in spite of the glitch which had cut him off mid *Mondays*). I know what Brian Adams meant when he called Bob a saint; that sort of focus and energy and generosity is rarely demonstrated.

Reflecting now, I feel so powerless and ashamed to think that even if we could have done it every year since with the same response, we would never solve the whole problem of famine in Africa, let alone Feed the World. It is even worse to realise that **'appeal fatigue'** would mean that response would tail off as familiarity meant declining income to charities. How often do we have to see the like of **Michael Buerk**'s reports to remind us that we are all accountable? All I can hope is that I remember that a little involvement in one day's Global Jukebox is not the end of my involvement in the big picture.

It was an extraordinary day and I am happy to have been a small part of the efforts of a business, usually so **slavishly** devoted to the pursuit of profit, doing something that felt useful for once. Thank you Bob Geldof, for that opportunity. And if you ever need a hand again, just say the word.

Neill Bayley

'appeal fatigue':   the fact that people become tired of charity appeals
Michael Buerk: the television reporter; see pages 32–33
slavishly: done without questioning

Extract 5

Memories of Glastonbury 2000

I knew the performance was going to have to be a great one from the moment I woke up. I had crawled out of our tent that morning and could hear the distant sound of `Concrete Jungle` being played — a favourite Bob Marley and the Wailers tune. Panic struck me — I thought I had missed the set. Then I was told they would be playing again later that afternoon, I relaxed. What other festival, apart from Glastonbury, would have the Wailers playing twice?

At two o'clock we set off for the stage they were due to be playing on. the Jazz Stage. As we approached, I could feel my heart going on a rampage. I could hear the beat of the music, once distant. becoming steadily louder, getting closer. They had already started, but I soon realised afterwards that we could have walked in at any point in the set and the initial feeling of the band starting to play and the greatness of it all would still have been buzzing through the crowd.

We weren't close to the stage, we were midway back and quite some way to the right-hand side. From here I could see the women — the `I Three` — all clad in long, straight, stripey dresses of green, red, yellow and black — the Rastafarian colours. One of them was standing centre stage at the microphone. She spoke to the crowd, the crowd that was full of tension. excitement, and the constant reggae beat keeping these feelings real. This alongside of the fact that you and everyone around you watching the performance was cherishing and holding on to their few moments with the legendary Wailers and, in their own way, with Marley himself. The tall, elegant figure at the microphone — in fact, Marley's wife — then addressed the crowd, announcing: `And now here's a tribute to our brother Bob Marley.`

This point for me was definitely the most memorable.

Tears filled my eyes, and yet I felt a stronger sense of happiness and freedom than I have ever done before. I wiped my eyes and saw that a taller figure had emerged on to the stage, a man with long, black hair, held back as dreadlocks. He too was wearing a long, robe-like garment, but his was white. The whole event was spectacular. It was easy to imagine that this man was Marley himself. Easier for me than some, I suppose, for I had missed the woman introducing him. I was so overcome with emotion. I had no idea who he was. He asked for 'positive vibrations' to be let loose through the crowd – another buzz and a cheer from the overwhelmed audience.

The moment they said their last words and left the stage, I knew that one thing had been shared throughout the crowd and probably the Wailers too. It was the most positively uplifting emotional rush I've ever hoped to experience.

Lucy O'Connor

Activities

1 **a** Bob Considine's account of the Joe Louis fight on pages 55–57 is written in a very informal, everyday style (a 'colloquial' style): the author uses slang words and verbs and adjectives which give an impression of speed. As you read, you can hear a commentator speaking these words. The style fits the subject matter because a report of a boxing match is fast and informal.

   Read the report again and, in pairs, pick out examples of this colloquial style. For example, where does Considine:

   - address the reader like someone talking excitedly to a friend?
   - use slang expressions such as 'guy', 'ball yard' and 'stew-bum'?
   - ask us to visualise the scene with expressions such as 'Louis was like this:'?
   - use striking comparisons (for example, to a drunk and to a shot-gun)?

   b Write your own account of a conflict that you have seen. It does not have to be a fight: it could be an argument, or a one-on-one sporting contest of some kind. Use a colloquial style, as Considine does.

2 **a** Look back at the description of the 1966 World Cup final (pages 58–60). Any step-by-step account of a sporting event has to use *adverbs of time*: words and phrases which let us know when things happened and in what order. For example, in the opening paragraph, Jason

Tomas tells us that trainer Harold Shepherdson approached the manager Alf Ramsay 'At the final whistle'.

In pairs, summarise what happened in the final part of the match, using the following adverbs of time from the report:

- 13 minutes from the end of normal time
- in the last minute
- before the start of extra time
- Ten minutes into extra time
- Deep into the last minute.

Notice that the writing is more interesting if the adverbs do not always come at the beginning of the sentence.

b Write a brief set of instructions for carrying out a task. It could be a recipe, for example, or instructions for putting up a tent or mending a puncture. Choose an activity which will give you the opportunity to practise using adverbs of time.

For example, you might use phrases such as:

First you need to . . . After a few minutes . . .
. . . when it has . . . Finally . . .

3 a Re-read the report of how Roger Bannister broke the four-minute mile (pages 61–64). Journalists writing news reports often find it useful to add helpful, informative phrases in brackets, or between commas or dashes. A phrase added in this way is called a *parenthesis*. (The plural term *parenthes***es** can also refer to the brackets themselves.) For example, in the first sentence, the reporter Jack Crump writes about 'Roger Gilbert Bannister, who was timed officially to run the distance in 3min 59.4sec'.

But, between commas, he adds the parenthesis '25-year-old medical student', to give us more information about the runner.

Find some other examples of parenthesis in the article. For example, where in the first two paragraphs does the writer:

- add information between dashes, about the sports ground where the race took place?
- include runners' nationalities, in brackets?
- add another runner's best time for the mile, between commas?

Look through some of the books you have at school to find other examples of parenthesis. Make a note of:

- the punctuation used (brackets, commas or dashes)
- what kind of information has been added.

b Imagine that you are a commentator reporting live on the race. Using the information that begins 'From the start' and ends, 'athletic president', write a commentary on the race.

c After live sporting events, the commentator often interviews those involved. Write some notes on the questions you would ask Bannister after the race, and on how you think he would respond.

4 a Re-read the two extracts on pages 65–68. When people describe an event, they often talk about the performers' qualities, or their own emotions. To do this they use *abstract nouns*. For example, Neill Bayley writes about the different performers' 'simplicity', 'power' *and* 'charisma', as well as the emotional 'wrench'; Lucy O'Connor talks about 'excitement', 'happiness' and 'freedom'.

Which three abstract nouns are used to label qualities of Bob Geldof's in Neill Bayley's account? List four abstract nouns to label the feelings you have when:

- watching a great sporting event
- listening to music.

b For Neill Bayley, Live Aid was not only an enjoyable event, but also a satisfying achievement, and one which made him think about the millions of people who did not have such an easy life. For Lucy O'Connor, seeing the Wailers perform live fulfilled a long-held ambition.

Write an account of an event which changed you in some way or really made you think. (It does not have to be a 'live' event that you experienced – you could write about a book you have read or a television programme you have seen.)

Alternatively, write about seeing a performer, sporting figure or sports team that you had always admired but had never seen live before.

In either case, choose abstract nouns carefully, in order to describe both the performers' qualities and the feelings that you experienced.

Comparing texts

5 **a** When you write a report of a big event, it is important to think about your purpose (the reason why you are writing it) and your audience (the people who are likely to read it). For example, your purpose might be to:

- entertain the readers
- inform them
- put forward an argument
- express personal feelings
- amuse people

and your audience might be:

- people who are interested in this special area (such as boxing or rock music)
- general readers who will read almost anything if it is interesting enough
- a small group of friends
- a teacher.

Look back at the reports in this section and, in pairs, try to decide what the purpose and audience was for each one. You might feel that some of the extracts have more than one purpose and more than one intended audience. Do any have the same purpose, or the same audience?

b In writing his account of the 1966 football World Cup final, Jason Tomas was not interested in just giving us a report of what happened on the pitch: he tells us about the reactions of the trainer and the manager, as well as the crowd, and also gives us an idea of the way the match has stayed in people's memories.

Write your own account of a 'big event'. It does not have to be something you attended in person – you could write about a sporting event, for example, or a rock concert that you have seen on television. But first decide what your purpose (or purposes) and audience are going to be. If you are not sure about how to plan your account, you could follow Lucy O'Connor's structure:

- introduction: what you expect and are anxious about before the event
- paragraph 2: approaching the stage or stadium
- paragraph 3: what you see first; the feelings of the crowd
- paragraph 4: focus on one particular performer or sportsperson
- paragraph 5: focus on a single moment
- conclusion: the feelings you are left with.

Section 6
War

This section contains eyewitness accounts taken from the First and Second World Wars. Some are by the soldiers, sailors and airmen themselves, recalling moments of terror or heroism. Others are not by the people who were actually fighting, but come from nurses and civilians who experienced the destruction of war at first hand, and were able to record its wastefulness. Read the introductions and extracts which follow, before working through the activities on pages 99–106.

Extract 1: Gas attack (page 78)

When we think of the First World War of 1914–1918, known as the Great War, most of the images are of trenches, wading in deep mud, and men 'going over the top'. But one group of people who lived through this daily horror were the nurses who tended the wounded. Most of them had lived ordinary lives at home, sheltered from violence and ugliness. For them, witnessing the suffering of the wounded was an experience that was to change their lives.

One of the most terrifying weapons to be used in the Great War was poison gas. Gas bombs were hurled into enemy trenches, where they exploded in a thick green fog and destroyed the soldiers' lungs or caused permanent blindness. Pat Beauchamp, who served as a nurse throughout the war, describes the immediate effects of one of the first of these gas attacks in the spring of 1915.

Extract 2: Nature and destruction (page 80)

The men and women who served at the front during the Great War were often moved by the awful contrast between the ugliness of the conflict and the beauty of nature in the fields and countryside around them. Siegfried Sassoon, one of the most famous writers to have fought in the Great War, kept a diary of his experiences. This is what he wrote on 23 May 1916.

Extract 3: The Flooded Trench (page 81)

Sassoon later recorded some of the horrifying sights he had seen in his autobiography, *Memoirs of an Infantry Officer*. Here he recalls leading a party which was carrying a heavy load of bombs through some trenches which had recently been captured from the Germans.

Extract 4: From a U-boat (page 83)

What thoughts go through a submarine commander's mind as he prepares to fire a torpedo at a ship which has no idea of his presence? Adolf von Spiegel was in charge of a German U-boat patrolling the seas in 1916. In this extract he describes his feelings as he looks through the periscope at the defenceless target.

Extract 5: The Zeppelin raids (page 86)

The Great War of 1914–1918 was the first time in which war could be seriously waged from the air. This meant that it was not just the men and women in the front line who were in danger, as British civilians found when parts of England were bombed by German Zeppelins – huge air-balloons built to serve the German navy. In the Second World War of 1939–1945, many cities suffered regular bombardment from the air during the blitz (from the German 'blitzkreig', meaning a violent attack).

James Cameron's collection of eyewitness accounts is unusual because it gives us the opportunity to view the raids from three quite different perspectives: that of the civilians who suffered the bombing; that of the pilots of the Royal Flying Corps and the Royal Naval Air Service who were sent up to fight the enemy airships; and that of a German Zeppelin crew member. Cameron begins by describing the birth of the 'dirigible' – an air-balloon which could be steered.

Extract 6: Entering a concentration camp (page 95)

The mass killing of Jews and other minorities in the Nazi concentration camps is one of the most awful atrocities in human history. When the camps were finally liberated by the Allied armies moving across Germany and occupied territories towards the end of the Second World War, people could hardly believe the sights they were faced with. A number of journalists travelled with the soldiers and sent back reports of their experiences.

Extract 7: Dropping the atomic bomb (page 98)

Towards the end of the Second World War, the United States used a new weapon which was to change the world's attitudes to warfare for ever. The first atomic bomb was dropped on the Japanese city of Hiroshima on 6 August 1945. An area of more than 10 square kilometres (4 square miles) was totally obliterated and nearly 80,000 people killed, with many more dying later from their injuries, including radiation sickness. This report appeared on the front page of the *Daily Telegraph* the following day.

Extract 1

Gas attack

Out of the queer green haze that hung over everything came an unending stream of **Tommies**, stumbling, staggering, gasping, all a livid green colour. One just reached our gatepost before he crumpled up. Five men supporting each other staggered along with a wounded comrade. The grass on each side of the *pavé* was thronged with those who could go no farther. It was the first gas attack.

We dashed to the kitchen and prepared large quantities of salt and water to help them vomit the poison. A heavy green liquid resulted, and we thanked God that they seemed relieved. No two men were affected in the same way, constitution playing an important part in resisting the gas of that time – none of them had respirators and they had been taken unawares in their sleep.

We noticed that those wearing the South African medal had clung to their rifles and equipment, but the young boys had left the trenches without theirs.

'Gawd, it's a woman,' breathed one, finding himself in a manger with Hutchinson bending over him.

'Smoked out like – rats, we were, by them – 'Uns' Ammunition columns began to come up and unload with feverish haste, and the shells were carried by hand through the yard to the guns; we improvised respirators with cotton-wool and weak **carbolic**

Tommies: British private soldiers (not officers); soldiers' slang
pavé: the roadway (French)
'Uns: 'Huns'; soldiers' slang for the Germans
carbolic: an antiseptic and disinfectant

solution for those going forward. Motor ambulances began to arrive, became entangled with ammunition wagons, disentangled themselves and finally each went their ways. We covered the men with blankets and placed them on hay in a shed to await collection. Hutchinson went inside the kitchen to prepare breakfast for our battery.

It was only then that I noticed that her face was blue and swollen and her eyes appeared to be twice their natural size. My own were giving me considerable pain and I supposed that I looked the same. 'Tear' shells were falling everywhere, and looking towards the front from where this hell had come, I saw the sun rising, blood-red above the gas, in one of the most perfect skies I have ever seen –

Pat Beauchamp, from *The Virago Book of Women and the Great War*

Extract 2

May 23

6.15 p.m.   On Crawley Ridge. A very still evening.

Sun rather hazy but sky mostly clear. Looking across to

Fricourt: trench-mortars bursting in the cemetery: clouds

of dull white vapour slowly float away over grey-green

grass with yellow buttercup-smears, and saffron of weeds.

Fricourt, a huddle of reddish roofs, skeleton village church –

tower white – almost demolished, a patch of white against

the sombre green of the Fricourt wood (full of German

batteries). Away up the hill the white seams and heapings of

trenches dug in the chalk. The sky full of lark songs.

Sometimes you can count thirty slowly and hear no sound of

a shot: then the muffled pop of a rifle-shot a long way off or a

banging 5.9, or our eighteen-pounder – then a burst of

machine-gun westward, the yellow sky with a web of whitish

filmy cloud half across the sun; and the ridges rather blurred

with outlines of trees; an airplane droning overhead. A thistle

sprouting through the chalk on the parapet; a cockchafer

sailing through the air a little way in front. Down the hill, and

on to the old Bray–Fricourt road, along by the railway; the

road white and hard; a partridge flies away calling; lush grass

everywhere, and crops of nettles; a large black slug out for his

evening walk (doing nearly a mile a month, I should think).

Siegfried Sassoon, *Diaries, 1915–1918*

Extract 3

The Flooded Trench

We were among the debris of the intense bombardment of ten days before, for we were passing along and across the Hindenburg Outpost Trench, with its belt of wire (fifty yards deep in places); here and there these rusty jungles had been flattened by tanks. The Outpost Trench was about 200 yards from the Main Trench, which was now our front line. It had been solidly made, ten feet deep, with timbered **fire-steps**, splayed sides, and timbered steps at intervals to front and rear and to machine-gun **emplacements**. Now it was wrecked as though by earthquake and eruption. Concrete strong-posts were smashed and tilted sideways; everywhere the chalky soil was **pocked and pitted** with huge shell-holes; and wherever we looked the mangled **effigies** of the dead were our **memento mori**. Shell-twisted and dismembered, the Germans maintained the violent attitudes in which they had died. The British had mostly been killed by bullets or bombs, so they looked more resigned. But I can remember a pair of hands (nationality unknown) which protruded from the soaked ashen soil like the roots of a tree turned upside down; one hand seemed to be pointing at the sky with an accusing gesture. Each time I

---

fire-steps: boards or ledges on which soldiers stood when firing
emplacements: solidly built platforms to which the machine-guns were fixed
pocked and pitted: scarred by holes
effigies: images (like statues)
memento mori: reminders of death (like the skulls sometimes carved on tombs)

passed that place the protest of those fingers became more expressive of an appeal to God in defiance of those who made the War. Who made the War. I laughed hysterically as the thought passed through my mud-stained mind. But I only laughed mentally, for my box of Stokes-gun ammunition left me no breath to spare for an angry guffaw. And the dead were the dead; this was no time to be pitying them or asking silly questions about their outraged lives. Such sights must be taken for granted, I thought, as I gasped and slithered and stumbled with my disconsolate crew. Floating on the surface of the flooded trench was the mask of a human face which had detached itself from the skull.

Siegfried Sassoon, *Memoirs of an Infantry Officer,* 1932

Extract 4

From a U-boat

The steamer appeared to be close to us and looked colossal. I saw the captain walking on his bridge, a small whistle in his mouth. I saw the crew cleaning the deck forward, and I saw, with surprise and a slight shudder, long rows of wooden partitions right along all the decks, from which gleamed the shining black and brown backs of horses.

'Oh, heavens, horses! What a pity, those lovely beasts!

'But it cannot be helped,' I went on thinking. 'War is war, and every horse the fewer on the Western front is a reduction of England's fighting power.' I must acknowledge, however, that the thought of what must come was a most unpleasant one, and I will describe what happened as briefly as possible.

There were only a few more degrees to go before the steamer would be on the correct bearing. She would be there almost immediately; she was passing us at the proper distance, only a few hundred metres away.

'Stand by for firing a torpedo!' I called down to the control room.

That was a cautionary order to all hands on board. Everyone held his breath.

Now the bows of the steamer cut across the

zero line of my periscope – now the forecastle – the bridge – the foremast – funnel –

'FIRE!'

A slight tremor went through the boat – the torpedo had gone.

'Beware, when it is released!'

The death-bringing shot was a true one, and the torpedo ran towards the doomed ship at high speed. I could follow its course exactly by the light streak of bubbles which was left in its wake.

'Twenty seconds,' counted the helmsman, who, watch in hand, had to measure the exact interval of time between the departure of the torpedo and its arrival at its destination.

'Twenty-three seconds.' Soon, soon this violent, terrifying thing would happen. I saw that the bubble-track of the torpedo had been **discovered** on the bridge of the steamer, as frightened arms pointed towards the water and the captain put his hands in front of his eyes and waited resignedly. Then a frightful explosion followed, and we were all thrown against one another by the concussion, and then, like **Vulcan**, huge and majestic, a column of water two hundred metres high and fifty metres broad, terrible in its beauty and power, shot up to the heavens.

'Hit **abaft** the second funnel,' I shouted down to the control room.

Then they fairly let themselves go down below. There was a real wave of enthusiasm, arising from hearts freed from suspense, a wave which rushed through the whole boat and whose joyous echoes reached me in the **conning tower**. And over there?

---

discovered: noticed
Vulcan: the Roman god of fire
abaft: behind
conning tower: the structure built on the top of a submarine

War is a hard task master. A terrible drama was being enacted on board the ship, which was hard hit and in a sinking condition. She had a heavy and rapidly increasing **list** towards us.

All her decks lay visible to me. From all the hatchways a storming, despairing mass of men were fighting their way on deck, grimy stokers, officers, soldiers, grooms, cooks. They all rushed, ran, screamed for boats, tore and thrust one another from the ladders leading down to them, fought for the lifebelts and jostled one another on the sloping deck. All amongst them, rearing, slipping horses were wedged. The **starboard** boats could not be lowered on account of the list; everyone therefore ran across to the **port** boats, which, in the hurry and panic, had been lowered with great stupidity either half full or overcrowded. The men left behind were wringing their hands in despair and running to and fro along the decks; finally they threw themselves into the water so as to swim to the boats.

Then – a second explosion, followed by the escape of white hissing steam from all hatchways and **scuttles**. The white steam drove the horses mad. I saw a beautiful long-tailed dapple-grey horse take a mighty leap over the **berthing rails** and land into a fully laden boat. At that point I could not bear the sight any longer, and I lowered the periscope and dived deep.

Adolf von Spiegel, *U-Boat 202*, 1919

---

list: tilt
starboard: the right-hand side of a ship
port: the left-hand side of a ship
scuttles: similar to a hatchway, but smaller
berthing rails: narrow pieces of wood attached to the sides of a ship

Extract 5

The Zeppelin Raids

It was Germany that gave birth to the airship, the big dirigible buoyant gasbag, in the early years of the century. By 1914 dirigibles had flown more than 100,000 miles and carried more than 10,000 passengers without casualty. Sometimes it chanced that military men joined the crews for training.

Honours fell to the designer, who gave his name to the airship: the Count Ferdinand von Zeppelin. But he had always seen these great things as having a grander destiny than pleasure cruising. He saw them as flying warships. They would be a new and invincible arm to Germany's growing war machine. They would not carry passengers; they would carry bombs.

Some months after war came in 1914 the **Kaiser** finally agreed that the Zeppelins – as they were now called – were to be used against Britain. A veteran of many of these raids was Kurt Dehn.

Kaiser: the ruler of Germany until 1918

KURT DEHN *We made a point of never approaching the coast until it was dark, because the communications system didn't exist in those days. So it was easily possible that nobody would know of the approach of a Zeppelin until he could hear the noise of the engine.*

GEORGE HARRIS *I thought to myself 'I don't know, I can hear something rhumm, rhumm, rhumm, rhumm, rhumm - like that you see'. And all about 2 or 3 seconds afterwards I could hear them coming nearer, and I thought to myself 'Well, I don't know. What is it? That's not an aeroplane,' I said to myself.*

What George Harris of Great Yarmouth had heard was the approach of the first Zeppelin over England – No. L.3., commanded by Kapitän-Leutnant Johann Fritze. It was about eight in the evening of 19 January 1915.

GEORGE HARRIS *I saw an object coming down, and all of a sudden I run towards my gal, what I was courting, and I said: 'I don't know, but I think that's coming this way.' Then there was this great explosion.*

That was a bomb exploding harmlessly on a lawn in Norfolk Square. A second bomb fell in Crown Road, and failed to go off. A third fell near Gordon Terrace, doing little damage.

But then a fourth bomb fell beside St Peter's Church, and it killed two people; they were Miss Martha Taylor, aged 72, and Samuel Smith, a 53-year-old shoemaker. They were Britain's very first air-raid casualties.

That evening two young girls stayed indoors at 5, Drakes Buildings. They were Gladys and Kathleen Goudge – the tellers of Britain's first bomb-story.

GLADYS GOUDGE *My mother went to what we called Daddy Goachers, on Victoria Road, to get the cough mixture, and she met Miss Taylor in there.*

Miss Taylor lived at 2, Drakes Buildings, and when they came away, my mother said Miss Taylor walked a bit slow, she hurried on in front and I can remember this door being flung open and the windows coming in: my mother being thrown on to the couch.

Miss Taylor was unfortunate – she got killed on the road. So if they'd kept together my mother would have been killed and all.

KATHLEEN GOUDGE *It happened just on the corner – just about a hundred yards away from here.*

GLADYS GOUDGE *That's where Mr Smith got killed too.*

KATHLEEN GOUDGE *Yes, Mr Smith had a cobblers shop just round the corner here and I suppose he came outside to see what was going on and he got killed.*

GLADYS GOUDGE *When you're children you soon get over it. Next morning we were fascinated to go through the rubbish of this opening to get out. You had to go in through the room, out the front, because there was too much debris.*

It was the Royal Naval Air Service which at first took the brunt of the defence against the Zeppelins. Flying was something new for the Navy. One of their pilots was a young Flight Sub-Lieutenant, Gerard Fane.

GERARD FANE *When the Zeppelins came, we had to concentrate on night flying. Originally, of course, flying at night was a sort of heroic business, and everybody thought you were marvellous. But it wasn't really as difficult as all that. But having gone up you had to do something when you got there.*

*We had a 12-bore paradox double-barrel shotgun with chain shot in one barrel and an **incendiary bullet** in the*

---

incendiary bullet: one which bursts into flames

other. You went up with that in the cockpit with a 20-lb bomb in your lap. You had to be high enough to get over it you see. But they were quite hopeless, and nobody really got a chance to use them.

They tried some things called LePrieur rockets. You had four rockets on each side of the aeroplane, lashed on to the **struts**. The theory was you dived at the thing and pressed the button and the rockets did the rest, but, unfortunately, they'd only got a range of about 50 yards, and they used to go just ahead of the aeroplane when you pressed the button.

You very soon caught up with them and so they were quite useless. It would be much cheaper to ram the Zeppelin and get a **posthumous V.C.** or something rather than waste money on the rocket.

KURT DEHN *In the Zeppelins, I don't think they even gave us a chair, because the 500 grams would have contributed towards the weight of another bomb. We were sitting on the chart table, if we were sitting at all.*

Looking forward was one of the two **N.C.O.s** for navigation and steering. Then there was a commanding officer standing somewhere around.

You had to be very exact and knowledgeable to get the ship exactly over the target, and so many so-called targets were not targets. They thought they were over, say, the estuary of the Thames, and in reality they were near Portsmouth.

By the autumn of 1915 there had been nineteen Zeppelin raids – four of them on London. Only St Paul's, Westminster Abbey and Buckingham Palace were forbidden targets.

---

struts: wooden bars on the wings

posthumous V.C.: a Victoria Cross (medal for bravery) awarded after a person has died

N.C.O.s: non-commissioned officers (men who had risen through the ranks to become officers)

Altogether 136 people had been killed in the random bombing of Britain. They were raids intended to bring Britain to her knees; but those who flew the Zeppelins knew that if they hit a town, let alone a specific target, it was more by luck than judgement.

KURT DEHN *It was very difficult, unless it was a clear night, because the Thames can't be boarded up. So once we had the Thames, of course, we had London. It is all rubbish to say this was the so-and-so building and we dropped our bombs over that building. I never believed a word of that. You were happy enough if you found London, and you were even happier if you could drop your bombs and go home as soon as possible.*

They weren't in much danger; the guns defending London were very few. In October 1915 seven aeroplanes were diverted from the European battle-front to operate from three make-shift airfields on the outskirts of the capital. There were only a handful of half-trained Royal Flying Corps pilots to fly them. One was eighteen-year-old John Slessor. He learned night-flying the hard way.

JOHN SLESSOR *Purely by chance, one of my few claims to fame is that I, by luck, happened to be the first chap to **intercept** an enemy aircraft over England. But it wasn't a very effective interception.*

*It was the ordinary old stick and string aeroplane, no guns, of course, and the **armament** was a ridiculous **Heath-Robinsonian device**. You took a little bomb in your hand; you put it through a hole in the floor of the aeroplane and it lit an electric contact and as it dropped out came a bunch of fish-hooks, and these were supposed to stick in the skin*

---

intercept: cut off

armament: weapons system

Heath-Robinsonian device: Heath Robinson was a cartoonist famous for drawing fantastic imaginary machines

of the Zeppelin, and it then burst into flames. The great snag of that was that it meant getting above the Zeppelin, and in those days it had a far higher rate of climb.

And I was sort of climbing to get my height and I suddenly saw this huge thing. It was enormous. Actually it was L.15 commanded by a fellow called Briethaupt.

Some years afterwards I gave him a couple of gins in the R.A.F. Club, and we swapped lies, and he had been doing exactly what I thought. He was lying with his engine off to – listening, you see. Then he heard my engine. That was an extraordinary sight, because you suddenly saw a string of sparks come out of the lower engines of his ship. He didn't move forward much, but I remember being absolutely staggered by the angle at which he climbed. This huge bulk slowly tipped up, and just went *phrr* and left me standing.

While I'd been in the air, one of the half dozen anti-aircraft guns available had arrived on the airfield, believe it or not, with a searchlight. The fellow in charge of this thing thought it would be a help if he switched on the searchlight; which he did; bang in my eye – in the fog. By the grace of God I somehow or other just ran into the turnip field at one end of the stubble and broke various parts of the aeroplane.

KURT DEHN *It was wonderful as long as you could fly in the dark. Then all of a sudden there would be searchlights far in the distance. They began searching for you, and then all of a sudden you were in the middle of the beam and there were six, seven, eight, twelve others focusing on you, and then the anti-aircraft would start shooting at you. You couldn't do much, because this six hundred feet long monster is not as moveable as a **Fokker**.*

Fokker: a make of German aircraft

From then on the casualties among these vast airships grew almost weekly, as defensive techniques improved. Zeppelin crews came to realise that a sortie over England was likely to end in destruction.

> KURT DEHN *Whenever I think of Zeppelins, I think of that moment of sunset when you realised in your thoughts — is it now goodbye sun, or is it au revoir? The alternative was: you would either sit in your mess room next morning and have your eggs and bacon, or your bones would be lying in one of the fields of England.*

James Cameron and others, *Yesterday's Witness*, BBC, 1979

Afterword:
The Zeppelins raided Britain on 51 nights over four years and dropped over 6,000 bombs. Five hundred British civilians and 40 per cent of the German crews were killed.

Extract 6

THE HORRORS OF BUCHENWALD

Germans Shocked

A CONDUCTED TOUR OF THE CAMP

From our Special Correspondent

WEIMAR.
Escorted by American military police, a thousand of the citizens of Weimar marched six miles through lovely country to the Buchenwald concentration camp yesterday.

There in groups of 100 they were conducted on a tour of the crematorium with the blackened frames of bodies still in the ovens and two piles of **emaciated** dead in the yard outside, through huts where living skeletons too ill or weak to rise lay packed in three-tier bunks, through the riding stables where Thulmann, the German Communist leader, and thousands of others were shot, through the research block where doctors tried new serums on human beings with fatal consequences in 90 per cent of the cases.

It was an experience they can never forget. Most of the women and some of the men were in tears as they moved from block to block. Many were crying bitterly. Some of the women fainted and could be taken no farther.

Substantial help of every kind has been rushed to the 21,000 prisoners in the camp when overrun by the **Third Army**, but men are

emaciated: abnormally thin
Third Army: part of the American forces

still dying at the rate of forty a day. Many are beyond human help. Doctors say this one will die to-day, that one to-morrow, and others may have a month to live – no more. Such is Nazism.

As I accompanied one group of Germans through the hut another victim died and his wasted white frame was lifted easily from the bunk where six other men still lay to the centre of the hut.

It is to the everlasting credit of the men at the camp that despite the dire continuous hunger, the children were not in too bad shape, though looking like little old men with yellow faces and sunken cheeks. Milk was brought in to children immediately. Also brought in in abundance were meat and vegetables from captured German stocks and 20,000 kilos of bread from German bakeries.

CAREFUL FEEDING
But the feeding had to be tackled carefully. Even so, after long malnutrition a number of inmates experienced stomach aches for the first day or two. They were fed mostly by the Germans with thin barley soup, and so the Americans have started with soup containing meat and vegetables which are gradually being increased. A start was made with 300 grammes of bread a day, but already it is up to 750.

The Nazis destroyed the camp water supply, but the Army has installed a water point and rationed supplies are available. Everyone in the camp is being dusted with D.D.T. powder, the inventor of which is believed at one time to have been an inmate here.

Among the inmates are 70 doctors of different nationalities. Not all are fit to work, but those able to are helping.

Walter Hummelshein, secretary in 1933 to Von Papen when he was chancellor, who has been a prisoner of the Nazis for four years, told me that four or five days after the bombing of the factory area of the camp last August, Thulmann was brought to the camp as far as the riding stables where he and nine other Communist leaders were shot. He was never an inmate and was not killed in a raid.

Manchester Guardian, 18 April, 1945

Extract 7

ALLIES INVENT ATOMIC BOMB: FIRST DROPPED ON JAPAN

2,000 TIMES THE BLAST-POWER OF R.A.F. 11-TONNER

Over 2,000 times the blast power of the largest bomb ever before used, which was the British 'Grand Slam,' weighing about 11 tons; and more power than 20,000 tons of **T.N.T.**

Yet the explosive charge is officially described as 'exceedingly small.' A spokesman at the Ministry of Aircraft Production said last night that the bomb was one-tenth the size of a 'block buster,' yet its effect would be 'like that of a severe earthquake.'

The first atomic bomb, a single one, was dropped on Hiroshima, a town of 12 square miles, on the Japanese main island of Honshu. Tokyo radio said that the raid was at 8.20 a.m. yesterday, Japanese time,

The Allies have made the greatest scientific discovery in history: the way to use atomic energy. The first atomic bomb has been dropped on Japan. It had:

T.N.T.: powerful high explosive

and that the extent of the damage was being investigated.

The official announcement yesterday of the existence of the bomb was made 16 hours after its first use. Late last night no report had been made on the damage done because it had been impossible to see the result through **impenetrable clouds** of dust and smoke.

EFFECT ON WAR AND PEACE

Statements were yesterday issued by Mr. CHURCHILL from Downing-street, by Mr. TRUMAN from the White House and by Mr. STIMSON, United States Secretary of War, giving an account of the research which led to the development of the new weapon; of the terrible fate awaiting Japan if she does not immediately yield; of the future use of atomic energy as a source of power and an instrument for keeping the world's peace.

In the Downing-street Statement Mr. CHURCHILL was quoted as saying: 'By God's mercy British and American science outpaced all German efforts. The possession of these powers by the Germans at any time might have altered the result of the war and profound anxiety was felt by those who were informed.'

Mr. STIMSON said the bomb would prove a tremendous aid in shortening the war against Japan. It had an explosive power that 'staggered the imagination.'

President TRUMAN described the results as the greatest achievement of organised science in history. The Allies had spent the sum of £500,000,000 on the 'greatest scientific gamble in history,' and had won.

If the Japanese did not now accept the Allies' terms, he said, they might expect 'a rain of ruin from the air the like of which had never been seen on this earth.'

The method of production would be kept secret, while processes were being worked out to protect the world from the danger of sudden destruction. Congress would be asked to investigate how atomic power might be used to maintain the future peace.

---

impenetrable clouds: clouds that could not be seen through

TEST FLASH WAS SEEN 350 MILES AWAY

◆

Impact Vapourised Steel Tower

FROM OUR OWN CORRESPONDENT
WASHINGTON, Monday.

The first test of the new atomic bomb took place at 5.38 a.m. on July 16 at the air base of Alamogordo, in a remote section of the New Mexico desert, the War Department disclosed to-day.

When the test was over the explosion had completely vapourised the steel tower on which the weapon was mounted. Eye-witnesses said that where the tower once had stood there remained only a huge sloping crater.

The explosion had such an impact that a blind girl near Albuquerque exclaimed, 'What was that?' when the flash of the test lighted the sky, even before the explosion was heard.

Daily Telegraph, 7 August 1945

Activities

1 a A number of the soldiers in the Great War
described its horrors in poetry. The most famous
of these soldier-poets was Wilfred Owen, who
was killed just before the war ended. In this
extract from one of his poems, he describes the
kind of gas attack which would have caused the
injuries witnessed by Pat Beauchamp. A group
of soldiers are trudging back to their trench;
they are so exhausted that they fail to hear the
gas-shells falling around them …

> *Gas! Gas! Quick, boys! – An ecstasy of fumbling,*
> *Fitting the clumsy helmets just in time;*
> *But someone still was yelling out and*
>   *stumbling*
> *And flound'ring like a man in fire and lime –*
> *Dim, through the misty panes and thick green*
>   *light,*
> *As under a green sea, I saw him drowning.*
>
> *In all my dreams, before my helpless sight,*
> *He plunges at me, guttering, choking,*
>   *drowning.*
> *(from 'Dulce et Decorum est')*

In pairs, take it in turns to read the extract
from the poem out loud. Then talk together
about the language. For example:

- What do *fumbling, clumsy,* and *stumbling* tell
  you about the condition of the men?
- Which verbs describe the way the soldiers
  become overcome by the gas?

- Which words tell us how Owen himself was affected by witnessing this gas attack?

b Write two or three paragraphs about the connections you can find between Wilfred Owen's description of the gas attack and Pat Beauchamp's account of its after-effects. For example:

- Which colour do they both repeat? Why do you think they both focus on this colour?
- How did the men come to be taken by surprise in each case? What protection were they supposed to have against gas? Why was that protection no use in either instance?
- What do both accounts tell us about the effects of this poison gas? Why was it so horrifying?
- Which words and phrases would you pick out, from the account and the poem, as most effectively conveying the horror of a gas attack?

2 **a** Look back at the two extracts written by Siegfried Sassoon on pages 80–82. In the first extract in this section, the nurse Pat Beauchamp focused on three colours to help her description: the green of the gas and its after-effects; the blue of the swollen face; and the red of blood. In the first of Sassoon's descriptions, the extract from his diary, he refers to many more colours. Which colour (the one referred to most) is associated with destruction? (Interestingly, it is not black.)

Draw a table. In the first column list the pleasant sounds that Sassoon mentions in his diary, and in the second, the contrasting sounds associated with war which he describes.

b Design a cover for an edition of Sassoon's *Memoirs of an Infantry Officer*, the book from which Extract 3 was taken. You could use some of the horrifying sights he describes in that extract, or you could base your design on the contrasting pictures of nature and destruction from his diary, with its interesting use of colours. By the side, write brief notes to explain the decisions you made about the design.

3 a The extract on pages 83–85 gives a fascinating insight into the ever-changing emotions of someone whose job in wartime is to kill and destroy. To understand these emotions better, make notes on the main things that happen in this episode and, next to each one, write down Adolf von Spiegel's feelings about it. For example, you might start off:

Event	The commander's feelings
First close-up sight of the steamer	He feels that it is a pity to have to destroy the horses

b There have been many dramatic films featuring submarine attacks. Try turning this account into a film screenplay. You will not have to make up any dialogue – what you need is all in the extract already. But you will have to describe (or sketch) the different shots that the viewer will see when watching the film. For example, you could begin like this:

Shot 1: a view through the periscope of the steamer. As the periscope turns, scanning the deck, the steamer's captain comes into view.

Shot 2: inside the U-boat: the commander is looking intently through the periscope.

4   a   James Cameron's collection of eyewitness reports (pages 86–92) provides us with different viewpoints on the same set of events. In order to compare them, draw up a table with the following headings:

- name of witness
- adult or child
- serviceman or civilian
- British or German
- flying or on ground
- what they did during a raid
- what they did afterwards.

Complete the table, then pick out between one and four points made by each of the six witnesses – choose the points which you think are the most interesting, and which will also highlight their different viewpoints about the Zeppelin raids. In pairs, discuss what these points tell you about the way different witnesses see the same event.

b   Pick an important moment from history (perhaps something you have been learning about at school). Construct an account like James Cameron's, in which you write your own introduction and linking passages, but also let four or five eyewitnesses from the time speak for themselves. Make sure you choose eyewitnesses who can give you different points of view: for example, if you chose the discovery of America, your eyewitnesses could include Christopher Columbus, Queen Isabella of Castile (who financed the voyage), someone who helped build the ship, a sailor and a Native American.

5 a In groups of four, share what you know about the historical background to the Nazi death camps. For example:

- Who built and ran them?
- What was their purpose?
- What did they look like?
- Which other camps have you heard about, apart from Buchenwald?
- Which people died in these death camps?
- How many are estimated to have died?

b Imagine you are one of the local German civilians who was forced to look round the camp after it had been liberated. Use the details from the article to write a letter to a close friend or relation telling them what you saw, and describe how you felt.

6 a There are two ways of describing an action. If we use the *active* form (or voice) of the verb, we focus on the person who is doing the action – Jim *tidied* the house every week. ('Jim' here is the *subject* of the sentence.) If we use the *passive* form, we focus more on the action itself – 'The house *was tidied* every week'. In this second sentence, we do not know who the tidier is.

Look at this sentence from the article on pages 96–98:

The first atomic bomb *has been dropped* on Japan.

Because the writer has used the passive, he does not have to say who dropped the bomb. If he had used the active, he would have had to write: *The Allies have dropped* the first atomic bomb on Japan.

Find the following uses of the passive in the article. Write each one down and, next to it, write out what the phrase might have looked like if the active had been used. You will have to guess at what the subject might have been in each case:

- the explosive charge *is officially described* as 'exceedingly small'
- The first atomic bomb, a single one, *was dropped* on Hiroshima
- The method of production *would be kept* secret
- Congress *would be asked* to investigate …
- … how atomic power *might be used* to maintain the future peace.

b Imagine you were a Japanese journalist in 1946. Write the front-page report of this raid from the Japanese point of view. Remember that you will see the whole incident quite differently from the way the English journalist did – you might think that the active form of the verb is better than the passive from your perspective. There will be some facts that you will not know, so part of your article will probably consist of questions.

Comparing texts

7 a In small groups, discuss what purposes the writers of the extracts in this section might have had when writing. Do you think they all expected their words to be so widely read, and for so long after the event they describe? Which ones do you think were written mainly to inform; which ones wanted to get a particular view across; which ones were mainly expressions of personal feelings? Can you think of any other purposes the writers might have had in mind?

b Talk in groups about the impact that each of these extracts had on you. Which one impressed you most? You might consider which of the extracts:

- Enabled you to picture the scene most effectively?
- Best conveyed the horrors of war?
- Most clearly illustrated war's wastefulness?
- Showed the effect of war on civilians?
- Portrayed the feelings of men and women in wartime?

What impact do you think they would have had at the time? Think about whether the reader might be:

- familiar with the scene
- expecting to read about it.

c Edith Wharton, another nurse, recorded this scene by the River Meuse, near to Verdun, one of the bloodiest of the battlefields in the Great War:

Picture this all under a white winter sky, driving great flurries of snow across the mud-and-cinder coloured landscape, with the steel-cold Meuse winding between beaten Poplars . . . a knot of mud-coloured military motors & artillery horses, soldiers coming and going, cavalrymen riding up with messages, poor bandaged creatures in rag-bag clothes leaning in doorways, & always, over & above us, the boom, boom, boom of the guns on the grey heights to the east.

Redraft this description so that it becomes a poem entitled 'Picture this...'. You could then add a further section, possibly based on the extract from Wilfred Owen's 'Dulce et Decorum est' (page 99).

d Write your own piece of war reportage. It should be about 100 words long. You will need to think carefully about this piece of writing before you begin – the following checklist might help you:

- Choose a conflict that you know something about already – for example, a war that you have studied at school.
- Decide which point of view you are writing from: are you a nurse or doctor tending the wounded; or a soldier; or a civilian caught up in the fighting? What nationality are you?
- What is your purpose in writing – do you want to inform, or persuade people to share a particular point of view, or just express your personal feelings?
- Who is your intended audience – readers of a newspaper, or people at home or in another country, or just yourself?
- What form are you going to write in? Are you going to record your experience in a diary or a letter, or write a newspaper article or put together a collection of eyewitness reports?

ALSO IN

Heinemann
New Windmills

Founding Editors: Anne and Ian Serraillier

Chinua Achebe Things Fall Apart
David Almond Skellig
Maya Angelou I Know Why the Caged Bird Sings
Margaret Atwood The Handmaid's Tale
Jane Austen Pride and Prejudice
J G Ballard Empire of the Sun
Stan Barstow Joby; A Kind of Loving
Nina Bawden Carrie's War; Devil by the Sea; Kept in the Dark; The Finding; Humbug
Lesley Beake A Cageful of Butterflies
Malorie Blackman Tell Me No Lies; Words Last Forever
Ray Bradbury The Golden Apples of the Sun; The Illustrated Man
Betsy Byars The Midnight Fox; The Pinballs; The Not-Just-Anybody Family; The Eighteenth Emergency
Victor Canning The Runaways
Jane Leslie Conly Racso and the Rats of NIMH
Susan Cooper King of Shadows
Robert Cormier We All Fall Down; Heroes
Roald Dahl Danny, The Champion of the World; The Wonderful Story of Henry Sugar; George's Marvellous Medicine; The BFG; The Witches; Boy; Going Solo; Matilda; My Year
Anita Desai The Village by the Sea
Charles Dickens A Christmas Carol; Great Expectations; Hard Times; Oliver Twist; A Charles Dickens Selection
Berlie Doherty Granny was a Buffer Girl; Street Child
Roddy Doyle Paddy Clarke Ha Ha Ha
Anne Fine The Granny Project
Jamila Gavin The Wheel of Surya
Graham Greene The Third Man and The Fallen Idol; Brighton Rock
Thomas Hardy The Withered Arm and Other Wessex Tales
L P Hartley The Go-Between
Ernest Hemmingway The Old Man and the Sea; A Farewell to Arms
Barry Hines A Kestrel For A Knave
Nigel Hinton Getting Free; Buddy; Buddy's Song; Out of the Darkness
Anne Holm I Am David
Janni Howker Badger on the Barge; The Nature of the Beast; Martin Farrell

Pete Johnson The Protectors
Jennifer Johnston Shadows on Our Skin
Geraldine Kaye Comfort Herself
Daniel Keyes Flowers for Algernon
Dick King-Smith The Sheep-Pig
Elizabeth Laird Red Sky in the Morning; Kiss the Dust
D H Lawrence The Fox and The Virgin and the Gypsy; Selected Tales
George Layton The Swap
Harper Lee To Kill a Mockingbird
C Day Lewis The Otterbury Incident
Joan Lingard Across the Barricades; The File on Fraulein Berg
Penelope Lively The Ghost of Thomas Kempe
Jack London The Call of the Wild; White Fang
Bernard MacLaverty Cal; The Best of Bernard Mac Laverty
James Vance Marshall Walkabout
Ian McEwan The Daydreamer; A Child in Time
Michael Morpurgo My Friend Walter; The Wreck of the Zanzibar;
The War of Jenkins' Ear; Why the Whales Came; Arthur, High King
of Britain; Kensuke's Kingdom; Hereabout Hill
Beverley Naidoo No Turning Back
Bill Naughton The Goalkeeper's Revenge
New Windmill A Charles Dickens Selection
New Windmill Book of Classic Short Stories
New Windmill Book of Fiction and Non-fiction: Taking Off!
New Windmill Book of Haunting Tales
New Windmill Book of Humorous Stories: Don't Make Me Laugh
New Windmill Book of Nineteenth Century Short Stories
New Windmill Book of Non-fiction: Get Real!
New Windmill Book of Non-fiction: Real Lives, Real Times
New Windmill Book of Scottish Short Stories
New Windmill Book of Short Stories: Fast and Curious
New Windmill Book of Short Stories: From Beginning to End
New Windmill Book of Short Stories: Into the Unknown
New Windmill Book of Short Stories: Tales with a Twist
New Windmill Book of Short Stories: Trouble in Two Centuries
New Windmill Book of Short Stories: Ways with Words
New Windmill Book of Short Stories by Women
New Windmill Book of Stories from many Cultures and Traditions:
Fifty-Fifty Tutti-Frutti Chocolate-Chip
New Windmill Book of Stories from Many Genres: Myths, Murders
and Mysteries

How many have you read?